Cooking W·I·T·H Wisdom

Wholesome, Delicious, Simple Recipes for Health Conscious People

Carlisle Press

WALNUT CREEK

Cooking Naturally — from the Amish Community

First Printing May 1997
Second Printing August 1997 (6m)
Third Printing April 1998 (5m)
Fourth Printing April 1999(3m)
Fifth Printing July 2001 (2m)
Sixth Printing December 2002 (2.5m)

Cover photography by Larry McBride, Dover, Ohio
Pen art by Charlene Kennell, Washburn, Illinois
Design and printing by Carlisle Printing, Walnut Creek, Ohio

ISBN
Spiral 0-9642548-7-5

Carlisle Press
WALNUT CREEK

2673 Township Rd. 421 · Sugarcreek, OH 44681

III

DEDICATION

To Dr. D. J. Scott and my wife Miriam, I respectfully dedicate this book. They have inspired me to take seriously the responsibility of eating wholesome foods. Foods that strengthen – not weaken, that build – not leave in ruins my health.

Marvin Wengerd

IV

PREFACE

Changing one's diet is easy – if you plan on changing for a few weeks, or even a couple months. But to change for an indefinite period of time or for your lifetime is another matter entirely. Perseverance is the key. Rarely do we lose our health in a week or month. Most always disease comes from prolonged eating habits that destroy the life cycle of our body's living cells – one at a time.

For me this life changing transition from the "normal" contemporary diet to a health conscious one was born of necessity.

For a full ten years of my life – from a youth of seventeen to a father with two children at twenty-eight, my day began and ended with pain. Pain that was medically diagnosed as Rheumatoid Arthritis. Medically incurable, I quickly succumbed to the standard treatment – pain killing, organ destroying drugs. Waking up each morning, my first painful steps led me to the medicine cabinet for my morning pain killer. One at noon and one at bedtime. The dose at bedtime was almost as important as the one in the morning. Without it sleep was fitful and morning stiffness was doubly severe. Walking, bending, and lifting movements that healthy people take for granted were endurance tests for me. Running was out of the question.

And so I lived for those years—never a day without pain—never a day without pain killers.

Then the change—the change that has literally transformed my life from that time forward. I spent fourteen days at Dr. D.J. Scott's fasting clinic in Strongsville, Ohio. No, I didn't "fast" on fruit or vegetable juices, it was water and only water for eleven long days (nights were included too!). Dr. Scott instilled in me the idea of allowing my body to tell me how and what to eat. He gave me "principles to eat by," and taught me ways in which food should never be combined. Mostly, though, I was on my own. Dr. Scott urged me to "listen" to my system.

"If you eat what is detrimental to your body it will let you know," he emphasized. And that's the way it worked.

Following the fast, I had two key things going for myself of which I was totally unaware. The first was that I had an almost new digestive system. One that was free of toxins and acids. My digestive system could readily signal to my brain the positive and negative messages regarding my food. It was no longer overworked and harrassed.

Secondly, I had to relearn eating. Old habits were not easily fallen into. Food that was artificially sweetened tasted unbearably sweet. Even the smallest amount of salt sent my taste palette reeling. Some of the foods I enjoyed prior to the fast had absolutely no appeal. For example, prior to the fast meatloaf was one of my favorites. I distinctly recall thinking on one of those eleven long days on water, that I can't wait to devour a hearty piece of meatloaf when I break my fast. That's not how it worked though. I had positively no desire for animal foods after my fast. And I have yet to eat my first piece of meatloaf, five years later.

Changing my diet though has not been a "piece of cake" as they say. Our family's diet was a serious consideration. Were they to eat as I did? The recipes in *Cooking With Wisdom* have been a valuable tool in the hand of Miriam, my capable wife who has "steered our diet ship" off it's course of sure destruction onto a new plane. A plane where diet decisions are not solely based on cost and taste but on nutritional value.

Along with the fact that I have yet to eat my first piece of meatloaf, I haven't taken one pain killing drug since I changed my diet. And what's most exciting is the fact that outside the first few months following the water fast I haven't experienced even the slightest arthritis pain.

That's our hope for you. You may need to make a few changes—like I had to—and that's not always easy. However, the rewards are not to be compared with a few small inconveniences. Good health is a result of God's blessing and following a few principles. Principles that—if followed, will do more than give you good health—it will simplify and beautify your whole life.

–Marvin Wengerd

VI

ACKNOWLEDGMENTS

A grateful acknowledgment to every person who shared their natural food recipes. The names are listed with respect to the amount of recipes contributed.

Mrs. Lloyd Miller
Rexford, MT

Mrs. Donald Schrock
Shelbyville, TN

Mrs. Daniel Weaver
Shreve, OH

Mrs. David Mazelin
Scottsville, KY

Mrs. Raymond Kuepfer
Millbank, Ontario

Mrs. Urie Miller
Shipshewana, IN

Mrs. Nathan Weber
Smithsburg, MD

Mrs. Ervin Miller
Hillsboro, WI

Mrs. J. Detweiler
Marion, KY

Mrs. Nolan Rhodes
Harrisonburg, VA

Mrs. Rudy Gingerich
Hazleton, IA

Mrs. Enos M. Bender
Springs, PA

Mrs. Phyllis Peters
Three Rivers, MI

Mrs. Abe Keim
Dundee, OH

Mrs. David King
Kinzer, PA

Mrs. Harold Steiner
Kinzer, PA

Mrs. Phillip Brenneman
Montezuma, GA

Mrs. D. R. Showalter
Harrisonburg, VA

Mrs. Aaron Coblentz
Sugarcreek, OH

Mrs. Abe Miller
Guthrie, KY

Mrs. Phillip Kropf
Apple Creek, OH

Mrs. Tobie Schmucker
New Haven, IN

Mrs. Ora Headings
Hughesville, MO

Mrs. Daniel Yoder
Hillsboro, WI

Mrs. Allen R. Bates
Glasgow, KY

Mrs. Gerald Rudolph
New Oxford, PA

Polly D. Borntrager
Amherst, WI

Mrs. David Rohrer
Myerstown, PA

Mrs. Allen Derstine
Apple Creek, OH

Mrs. Mahlon Mast
Kalona, IA

Mrs. Vernon Troyer
Plain City, OH

Lillian Mast
Marion, KY

Mrs. Kenneth Steiner
Barwick, Ontario

Mrs. Alvin Graber
Kalona, IA

Mrs. Roy Miller
Fredericktown, OH

James M. Stauffer
Ephrata, PA

Mrs. Edwin Rissler
New Enterprise, PA

Mrs. Milo Hershberger

Mrs. Jake Yoder
Fredericksburg, OH

Mrs. Earl Huber
Knox City, MO

Mrs. Lester Miller
Holmesville, OH

Mrs. John Culp
Middlebury, IN

Mrs. Glen Beidler
Freeburg, PA

Mrs. A. Wengerd
Navarre, OH

Mrs. Sam C. Miller
Fredericksburg, OH

Mrs. Samuel Hilty
Berne, IN

Mrs. Roy Derstine
Apple Creek, OH

Mrs. Paul Habegger
Scottsville, KY

Mrs. Marvin Wengerd
Sugarcreek, OH

A special acknowledgment goes to Martha Schlabach and Carol Durstine for the initial compilation of these recipes.

VII

TABLE

OF

CONTENTS

Breads 1

Breakfasts 23

Main Dishes 39

Salads and Dressings 77

Cookies 95

Cakes 117

Pies 139

Desserts 149

Ice Cream and Frozen Desserts 163

Wholesome Snacks 171

Yogurt 181

Food Preservation 185

Miscellaneous 199

Natural Food Resources 209

Index 217

▾ *This symbol is used throughout this volume denoting recipes for persons with Candida.*

These recommendations are not intended to replace the advice of your physician.
The publishers make no guarantees, express or implied.

MEASUREMENT

EQUIVALENTS

1 stick (1/4 lb.) butter = 1/2 cup

1 cup buttermilk =
    1 or 2 Tablespoons vinegar with sweet milk to fill cup

1 package active dry yeast = 1 T.

1 package plain gelatin = 1 T.

1 lb. butter = 2 cups

pinch and dash = 1/8 tsp.

3 teaspoons = 1 Tablespoon

16 Tablespoons = 1 cup

1 cup = 1/2 pint

2 cups = 1 pint

2 pints (4 cups) = 1 quart

4 liquid quarts = 1 gallon

16 ounces = 1 pound

5 1/2 Tablespoons = 1/3 cup

4 Tablespoons = 1/4 cup

8 Tablespoons = 1/2 cup

10 2/3 Tablespoons = 2/3 cup

12 Tablespoons = 3/4 cup

14 Tablespoons = 7/8 cup

1 pound cornmeal = 3 cups

1 pound raisins = 3 cups

1 pound rice = 2 cups

breads

BREADS

Wheat flours vary depending on how coarsely or finely it is ground, and also on how old it is.

OUR BEST WHEAT BREAD

Put into large bowl:

3 c. warm water   2 T. yeast

1/2 c. sorghum, maple syrup, or honey

2 t. salt

Mix in:

1 c. oatmeal   6 to 7 c. ground wheat

Beat 100 times and let set where it is good and warm for an hour or so, beating down a time or two.

Beat in 1 egg and 2 T. oil. Add 3 good cups of bread flour. Get right in the dough with your hands and mix really well. It will be a sticky mess, but makes better bread!

This dough will be very soft. Try to oil bottom of bowl now, and also top of bread dough. Let rise, Punch down. Let rise again. Put in pans. Let rise a bit over double (not much) and bake.

Note: Keep dough nice and warm.

LIGHT AND CRUSTY BREAD

Mix:

12 c. whole wheat pastry flour (makes lighter bread)

4 c. whole wheat bread flour

1 c. bran   1 T. salt

Stir:

1 1/2 c. warm water   3 T. yeast

1/2 T. blackstrap molasses

Let set to sponge for 10 minutes.

5 c. warm water   1/4 c. honey

Add water, honey, and yeast mixture to above flour mixture. Stir well. Knead about 10 min. Pour 2 T. oil on hands and knead into dough. Place in bowl and cover. Let rise 15 min. and punch down. Let rise 1 hr. and punch down. Let rise 30 min. and shape into 6 large or 8 small loaves. Place in greased pans and let rise 30 min. Bake at 350° for 25 to 30 min. Reduce to 225° for 30 min. Remove from pans and cool on rack.

WHOLE WHEAT BREAD

Dissolve 1 T. yeast in 3 1/2 c. warm water.

1 T. salt

1 T. vinegar	8 to 9 c. whole wheat flour
2 T. blackstrap molasses	2 T. lecithin
1/4 c. safflower oil	1/2 c. honey

Mix altogether with yeast mixture. Let rise, punching down every 20 min. for 3 hrs.

Divide into 4 bread pans. Let rise 1 hr. Bake at 350° for 30 min.

CAROL'S WHOLE WHEAT BREAD

3 T. yeast	3 T. molasses
3 c. water	1 1/2 T. salt
3 c. milk	2 or 3 eggs*
9 T. butter	2 T. lecithin granules
5 T. honey	12 to 14 c. whole wheat flour*

Dissolve yeast in 1 1/2 c. of the water. Heat the rest of the water, milk, and butter together until the butter is melted. Put honey, molasses, and salt in a large bowl. Pour a little of the above heated mixture into the bowl and stir to dissolve. Add flour, 2 c. at a time, alternately with the heated mixture, making sure you fluff the flour before measuring. Stir dough well between each addition. After you have 8 to 10 c. of flour in, add the eggs and lecithin. Add dissolved yeast and rest of flour, 2 c. at a time, mixing well between additions. After all ingredients are mixed, knead 5 min. or so. Set in a warm place and cover lightly with a towel. Let rise until double.

When double in bulk, punch down dough and turn over. Let rise until double again. Divide dough into 5 equal parts. Shape into loaves and put into pans. Let loaves rise until double. Bake at 350° for 30 min. Makes 5 loaves.

*Amount of eggs and flour depends on texture of dough and humidity in the air. You don't want the dough too heavy.

Freshly ground is of course best, for wheat flour is as perishable as milk. If you need to store it, do so in the refrigerator. Having your own grinder and grinding grains as needed is ideal.

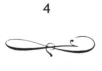

BREADS

Bread flour is made from hard wheat, while pastry flour is made from soft wheat. If in a bind, bread flour may be used for pastries. They tend to be a little more heavy.

For variation, try adding sesame seeds to your bread dough. Roll them in with a rolling pin.

EASY NO-KNEAD WHOLE WHEAT BREAD

Combine in large mixing bowl:

3 c. whole wheat flour	1 T. salt
1/4. c. honey	1 T. dry yeast

Heat in saucepan until very warm (120° to 130°):

2 c. water	
2 c. milk	1/2 c. oil

Add to dry ingredients:

warmed liquids	3 eggs

Blend at low speed until moistened. Beat 3 min. at medium speed. Stir in by hand no less than 6 c. whole wheat flour. Use enough flour to form a stiff batter. Cover and let rise until double. Make sure it doesn't rise any more than this. Stir down and spoon into 2 greased 9" x 5" bread pans. Pierce loaves with a fork. Bake immediately at 375° for 35 to 40 min. Remove from pans and cool on rack.

100% WHOLE WHEAT BREAD

1/3 c. sorghum or honey	2 c. lukewarm water
1 T. lecithin	2 t. salt
1 T. oil	6 c. whole wheat flour
1 T. yeast	

Dissolve yeast in warm water. Add oil, lecithin, salt and molasses or honey. Add the flour slowly, mixing in well. When it becomes too stiff to stir with a spoon turn out onto a well floured surface and knead in the rest of the flour (as much as you need). Put in a greased bowl; cover, and let rise until double. Punch down. Divide into equal parts; flatten with rolling pin. Shape into loaves and place in greased pans. Let rise till almost double. Bake at 300° for 30 minutes.

SWEDISH RYE BREAD (2 loaves)

1 3/4 to 2 c. milk
3 T. honey
1 1/2 T. shortening
1 t. caraway seed
4 c. wheat flour

2 T. molasses
1 pkg. yeast
2 t. salt
1 c. rye flour

Scald milk and cool. Add honey, molasses, and yeast and let stand 10 min. Add shortening, salt, caraway seed, and enough flour to make a smooth elastic dough. Knead until smooth and dry. Rye dough should be stiffer than white dough. Place in lightly greased, deep pan. Turn once to grease, cover, and let set in warm place (85°) until double, or about 2 hrs. Divide dough into 2 equal pieces and let rest 15 min. before shaping into loaves and placing in greased pans.

MULTI-GRAIN BREAD

Combine:
1 1/2 c. cornmeal
1 c. oatmeal
1/2 c. honey

2 1/2 T. salt
3/4 c. safflower oil

Pour 6 c. boiling water over this mixture. Cool to lukewarm and add:
6 T. yeast dissolved in 1 1/2 c. warm water
6 beaten eggs
3 c. rye flour

Finish to kneading consistency with approximately 14 to 15 c. whole wheat flour. Knead about 8 to 10 minutes. Let rise twice. Put in bread pans and let rise again. Bake at 350° for 30 to 35 minutes. Makes 9 loaves.

Adding 1 T. of soy lecithin to two loaves of bread dough will act as a preservative and make a more tender crust. Lecithin is available at natural food stores in granular or liquid form.

BREADS

6

Oatmeal or any cooked or left-over warm cereal improves the texture of bread and helps it stay moist longer. You will need to reduce the amount of liquid. Raw cereals can be soaked in the amount of liquid asked for in the recipe.

OATMEAL BREAD

3 c. hot water	2 T. salt
2 c. quick oats	3/4 c. oil
1 c. honey	3 T. yeast in 1 c. warm water
4 eggs	2 c. wheat flour

Pour hot water over oatmeal and set aside to cool. Beat all other ingredients together, making sure everything is just lukewarm before adding yeast mixture. Work in 9 c. more flour to make a nice spongy dough (not sticky). Grease top and let rise twice after kneading it. Bake at 400° for 10 min., lower to 350° for 25 to 30 min. Makes 5 to 6 loaves.

RICE BREAD

Bring 6 c. water and 2 c. brown rice to a boil. Reduce heat and simmer until soft. Cover and let set 5 min. Mash with potato masher.

Add:

2 c. water	3/4 c. psyllium seeds
1 1/2 T. salt	1 c. flax seeds
2 T. grated onion	3/4 c. sesame seeds
3 T. parsley	3 c. cornmeal
1 1/2 t. garlic	2 c. wheat bran
1 c. oat bran	3 c. whole wheat flour

Knead until dough is not sticky, adding more flour as needed. Shape loaf the size of your bread pan by rolling and patting. Place in greased pan. Bake at 150° for 1 hr., at 250° for 1 hr., and at 300° for 1 hr. Remove from pan and brush with oil. Slice *thin* while still warm. Package and freeze.

Note: This is very good toasted but breads should not have a sticky texture. It should be fairly dry but not crumbly. Don't give up if it doesn't turn out right the first time. If it gets too doughy, you may need to add some cornmeal.

BARLEY BREAD

1/2 c. molasses
1 t. baking soda
1 1/2 c. barley flour

1 1/2 c. water
1 1/4 c. fine barley flakes

 Mix all ingredients. Pour into a well greased bread pan. Bake at 350° for 45 min. to 1 hr. Makes 1 loaf.

PLUCKETS

1 c. milk
3 T. honey
3/4 t. salt
1/3 c. butter

1 heaping T. yeast
3/4 t. cinnamon
3 eggs, beaten
4 to 4 1/2 c. wheat flour

 Scald the milk and add the honey, butter, and salt. When lukewarm, add yeast (which has been dissolved in 1/4 c. lukewarm water), cinnamon, eggs, and flour, to make a stiff dough. The dough should be fairly sticky. When kneading, use butter on hands to work it. Cover and let rise until double in bulk.

 Roll the dough into small balls the size of walnuts, and dip into the following mixture:

1/2 c. butter, melted
3 t. cinnamon

1/2 c. honey

 Roll each ball into ground nuts and pile loosely into ungreased angel food cake pan, and let rise again for 25 to 30 min. (Do not use pan with removable bottom.) Bake at 375° for 10 min., then decrease heat to 350° and bake until brown.

 These are best when served warm, but may be wrapped in tin foil to reheat before serving.

 The buns will stick together and that's the way you serve them. Everyone plucks their bun from the central supply.

 Note: If any syrup is left, it may be poured on top of dough in tube pan.

You can make your own bread croutons by cutting old bread into small squares. Season to taste and toast in oven until hard.

8

BREADS

O nion, basil, dill, and oregano are good in bread.

HOVIS BREAD

1 1/2 c. whole wheat flour
1/2 c. rye flour
2 1/2 t. baking powder
1/2 t. salt

1/2 tsp. baking soda
3 T. sorghum
1 T. canola oil
1 3/4 c. soy milk

Mix together and bake in a loaf pan for one hour at 350°. Good hot or cold.

This can be a quick substitute for regular bread when there is no time to mix up a batch of yeast bread.

DELICIOUS ROLLS

Mix and let set 10 minutes:
1 T. dry yeast
3/4 c. lukewarm water

1 T. honey

Scald 1 c. milk and add:
1/2 t. salt
2 T. honey

4 T. butter

Add this to first part when milk has cooled to lukewarm, then add:
1 egg

1 t. vanilla

Knead in:
6 c. whole wheat flour (more or less)

Let rise until double in size. Fold down and let rise again. Roll dough out and spread like a piece of bread with butter and honey. Sprinkle with cinnamon. Roll together and cut. Let rise in greased pans until double in size. Pour milk or cream over rolls before baking at 350° for 30 minutes.

QUICK AND LIGHT DINNER ROLLS

3 c. warm water	1 T. oil
1/4 c. sorghum	2 T. yeast

Stir and let set to sponge.

1 c. bran	1 3/4 t. salt
2 c. whole wheat flour	

Beat into above. Add 2 c. whole wheat flour. Beat well. Add 2 c. whole wheat pastry flour. Beat well. Add 1 c. whole wheat flour. Knead into bread.

Cut into desired size, using more flour as needed. Shape into rounds and place on tray. Bake at 400° for 20 min., then at 300° for 10 min. Serve warm or cold, or freeze.

OATMEAL BUNS

2 c. warm water with 2 T. yeast

After yeast dissolves, add:

1/2 c. honey	2 t. salt
2 beaten eggs	6 T. oil
4 to 6 c. flour	1 1/2 c. oatmeal

Mix altogether as you do bread and let rise 2 hrs. Shape into rolls and let rise again. Bake at 350° for 25 to 30 min.

Note: Here is a good way to use up leftover cooked oatmeal.

CORNMEAL BISCUITS▼

2 c. flour (1 cornmeal and 1 mixture of wheat, rye, or barley)	
1/4 c. oil	1 t. salt
3 1/2 t. baking powder	3/4 c. water

Heat oven to 400°. Mix flour, salt, and baking powder. Stir in oil with fork, then add water. Sprinkle with flour and knead. Roll out *thick*. Sprinkle with cornmeal. Bake 10 min. Makes 12 biscuits.

When substituting cooked cereals for flour, reduce other liquids. Soak raw cereals in the amount of liquids specified in your recipe.

BREADS

Stoneground whole wheat flour is made from high protein, hard red spring wheat. It contains the gluten necessary for baking yeast bread; etc., and is most preferable in making noodles and pasta.

Flours milled from soft winter wheat have a lower protein content and are more suitable for baking cakes, pastries, etc.

BUTTERMILK BISCUITS

Mix together:

2 c. whole wheat flour	1 t. baking soda
1/2 t. salt	

(Use finely ground whole wheat flour and stir well to lighten.)

Cut in 1/2 c. butter and add 1 c. buttermilk.

Mix well, but do not overmix. Pat into 3/4 inch thickness on floured surface. Cut biscuits and, if you wish, dip in melted butter. Bake at 425° for 15 to 20 minutes.

GLUTEN-FREE BISCUITS▾

1/2 c. brown rice flour
1/4 c. millet (or Quinoa flour)
1/4 c. buckwheat flour (or soy flour)
1/4 c. canola oil (or butter)
1 T. sesame seeds
1/2 t. baking soda
1/4 t. celery salt, salt, or other desired seasoning
1/2 c. soy milk
1/2 c. finely grated carrots (optional)

Blend dry ingredients. Add wet ingredients and stir until mixed. Drop by teaspoon onto greased cookie sheet. Bake at 400° for 10 to 15 min.

Note: These are drier and more crumbly than with gluten grain flours.

BRAN MUFFINS▾

1 c. wheat bran	3/4 c. water
3/4 c. wheat flour (or your choice)	1/4 c. oil
1/2 t. salt	1 egg
1/2 t. baking soda	

Mix and bake in greased muffin tins at 425° for 20 min.

BRAN MUFFINS

Combine:

3/4 c. wheat flour	1/2 t. baking soda
1 c. oat bran	2 T. honey
1 1/4 t. salt	

Add:

1/4 c. molasses	1 c. buttermilk
2 T. melted butter	1 egg

Stir just to moisten. Fill well greased muffin tins 2/3 full. Bake 20 to 25 min. at 350°.

FAVORITE BRAN MUFFINS

2/3 c. bran	1 beaten egg
1 1/4 c. wheat flour	1/4 c. oil
1/2 c. toasted wheat germ	1/8 c. molasses
1/4 t. salt	1/4 c. honey
1 1/4 t. baking soda	1 c. buttermilk
1/2 c. boiling water	

In bowl, combine dry ingredients. Combine remaining ingredients and mix with dry ingredients. Spoon batter into greased muffin tins, filling 2/3 full. Bake at 350° for 20 to 25 min. Yields 1 dozen.

Variation: 1/2 t. carob powder, 1/2 t. cinnamon, and 1/2 t. ginger may be added instead of molasses.

Note: Recipe may be doubled and stored in refrigerator for up to 1 month to be used as needed.

BREADS

If you have Lifetime cookware, try the dry moist method for baking quick breads, biscuits and muffins. The lower baking temperature is much better for your oils and grains. The breads are not as dry this way, either.

BREADS

Muffins will slide right out of tin pans if the hot pan is first placed on a wet towel.

CINNAMUFFINS

1/4 c. oil	1 1/2 t. baking powder
1/4 c. honey	1 1/2 t. cinnamon
1/4 c. molasses	1/8 t. cloves
1 1/2 c. wheat flour	1/2 t. salt
1 c. unsweetened applesauce	1/2 t. baking soda
1/2 c. raisins	

Preheat oven to 375°. Grease a 12-cup muffin pan. Mix oil, honey, molasses, and applesauce. Sift dry ingredients. Stir together wet and dry ingredients and add raisins. Drop into muffin cups and bake 18 to 20 min.

CORNMEAL MUFFINS

Beat:

1/3 c. oil	1/2 c. honey
2 eggs	1 1/2 c. water or milk

Stir these dry ingredients together and add to above liquid mixture, stirring just enough to blend:

1 1/2 c. wheat flour	1 1/2 c. cornmeal
4 t. baking powder	1/2 t. salt

Bake at 400° for 15 to 20 min.

ORANGE OATMEAL MUFFINS

2 c. whole wheat flour	4 1/2 t. baking powder
1/2 t. baking soda	1/2 t. salt
1 1/2 c. oatmeal	1/2 c. maple syrup
1 orange, finely diced	1 c. water
2 beaten eggs	2 T. butter

Stir together dry ingredients and set aside. Mix maple syrup and orange and set aside. Combine eggs with butter, orange, and water. Mix well with dry ingredients. Pour into greased muffin tins. Bake at 350° for 30 minutes.

WHOLE GRAIN PUMPKIN MUFFINS

1 1/4 c. wheat flour or flour mix
1/2 t. cinnamon
1/2 c. toasted wheat germ   1/2 t. salt
2 1/2 t. baking powder   1/2 t. nutmeg
  Mix and add:
1 1/2 T. honey
2 egg whites, beaten until frothy
3/4 c. milk   1/4 c. oil
1/2 c. pumpkin   1 t. vanilla
  Stir, just until moistened. Bake at 400° for 20 to 25 min. Makes 12 muffins.

APPLE RAISIN OATMEAL MUFFINS

1 c. wheat flour or flour mix   3 t. baking powder
1 c. quick oats   1/2 t. salt
2 t. cinnamon   1 t. nutmeg
  Mix and add:
1 beaten egg   3/4 c. milk
2 T. honey   1/2 c. oil
1 c. chopped apples   1 c. raisins
  Bake at 400° for 15 to 20 min. Makes 12.
  Note: We are very fond of these muffins eaten like cornbread.

Wheat flours can vary, depending on how finely or coarsely they are ground or how old it is. You may wish to add or subtract to the amount the recipe asks for to give the dough the right consistency.

BREADS

Try adding shredded vegetables, fruit, nuts or seeds to breads, biscuits and muffins. Carrots, squash, beets, onions, celery seed, salt, sesame seeds, sunflower seeds, figs, dates, raisins, apples or applesauce can be used. Use your imagination! Or try adding black strap molasses (in small amounts) to baked goods.

CARROT MUFFINS

3 c. wheat flour	1 t. baking soda
2 t. baking powder	1/2 t. salt
1 c. grated carrots	1 t. cinnamon
1/4 c. honey or molasses	1/3 c. oil
2 eggs, beaten	1 1/2 c. milk

Sift dry ingredients. Add other ingredients, stirring only until mixed. Fill greased muffin tins or drop onto cookie sheets. Bake 20 min. in 400° oven.

Note: We like them warm with tea or cereal.

BANANA MUFFINS

In blender, mix:

1 egg	1/3 c. oil or butter
1/2 c. honey	1 large banana or 2 small

In bowl, mix:

1 1/2 c. barley flour	1 t. baking soda
1 t. baking powder	

Mix together and pour into muffin tin. Bake at 350° for 25 to 30 min. or until golden.

HEALTHY MUFFINS▾

(no sugar, no salt, no shortening)

2 c. whole wheat flour	2 c. buttermilk or skim milk
2 c. bran (your choice)	1/2 c. frozen apple juice
1 t. baking soda	concentrate
1 t. allspice	2 egg whites
1/2 t. vanilla	

Sift flour, baking powder, baking soda, and spices in bowl. Add remaining ingredients and fold in stiffly beaten egg whites last. Bake 20 minutes at 400°.

QUICK MUFFINS

1 to 3 c. cooked cereal
   Add:

3 eggs	2 T. oil
1/2 c. honey	1/2 t. salt

1/2 c. sour milk or yogurt

   Beat, then add 1 1/2 t. baking soda and 2 to 3 c. flour to make a batter like cake. Bake 12 to 15 min. at 400° in muffin tins.

   Note: This recipe is a good way to use up leftover oatmeal or any cooked grain cereal.

ORANGE NUT BREAD

   Combine:

1 1/2 c. water	3/4 c. honey
3 t. salt	

   Boil 10 min. Cool. Add milk to juice of 3 or 4 oranges to make 3 cups.

5 eggs, beaten	4 1/2 c. wheat flour
6 t. baking powder	3/4 c. oil
3/4 t. baking soda	1 1/2 c. nuts
	(raisins may be added instead)

   Add juice to beaten eggs. Next, add oil, then honey water. Blend in dry ingredients and add nuts. Bake in loaf pans at 350° for 50 to 60 min. Yields 4 loaves.

BREADS

A stale loaf of bread tastes almost fresh if you wrap it in a wet towel, set it on a pan, and bake in a slow oven until towel is almost dry.

BREADS

BANANA BREAD

6 T. butter	3 mashed, ripe bananas
1/2 c. honey	1 t. salt
3 eggs	2 t. baking soda
2 t. vanilla	1/4 t. nutmeg
3 t. cold water	1 1/2 t. cinnamon
1 c. wheat flour	1/2 c. ground nuts

Cream the butter and honey. Add vanilla and eggs. Sift the dry ingredients together. Add alternately with bananas and water. Add nuts and mix well. Pour into a loaf pan. Bake at 350° for 1 hr. or until a wooden toothpick inserted in the center comes out clean.

PUMPKIN BREAD▾

(no sugar)

2 c. pumpkin	1 c. chopped nuts or sunflower seeds
4 eggs, slightly beaten	1 c. raisins
2 1/2 c. whole wheat pastry	1/4 t. cloves
2 t. baking soda	2 t. cinnamon
1 c. 7 grain cereal or cracked wheat cereal	
2/3 c. hot water	1 c. oil

Beat eggs. Add pumpkin, spices, and baking soda. Mix and add remaining ingredients, except nuts and raisins. Fold nuts and raisins in last. Can be put into cake pans or bread pans. Bake 1 hr. at 350° or until done.

Optional: If sweetener is preferred, you may add 1/2 c. honey or unsulfured molasses and decrease water to 1/2 c.

PUMPKIN BREAD

1 1/2 c. honey
4 eggs
1 c. oil
2 c. pumpkin
1/3 c. water
3 1/2 c. rice flour or wheat flour
1/2 c. raisins
1 t. baking powder

1 1/2 t. baking soda
1 t. cinnamon
1 t. nutmeg
1 t. salt
1 t. vanilla

1/2 c. chopped nuts

   Pour into 2 small loaf pans. Bake at 350° for 40 to 45 minutes.

ZUCCHINI BREAD

3 eggs
1 c. oil
1 c. honey
3 t. vanilla
2 c. grated zucchini

3 c. wheat flour
1 t. baking soda
3 t. cinnamon
1/4 t. baking powder
2/3 c. chopped nuts

   Mix oil, honey, vanilla, and grated zucchini. Mix lightly, but well. Add dry ingredients. Mix until blended, then add nuts. Pour into 2 greased bread pans. Bake at 325° for 1 hr. Remove and cool on rack.

DELICIOUS QUICK BREAD

1 1/2 c. flour
1/4 c. brown rice flour
2 T. soy flour
2 T. arrow root flour
2 1/2 t. baking powder

1/2 t. Vege-sal
1/2 t. baking soda
3 T. sorghum
1 T. Canola oil
1 3/4 c. water

   Mix together and bake in a loaf pan (oiled) for 1 hr. at 350°. This is a quick substitute for regular bread. Delicious!

BREADS

A cooked, mashed potato adds moisture to whole grain breads.

BREADS

To enhance the texture of bread, try adding oatmeal or any kind of cooked or soaked cereal. Your bread will also stay moist longer.

APPLE CORN BREAD

3/4 c. corn meal	3/4 t. salt
3/4 c. wheat flour	1 T. honey
3 t. baking powder	3/4 c. milk
2 T. oil or melted butter	2 t. vanilla
1/4 t. ground cloves	1 t. cinnamon
2 c. diced apples	1 beaten egg

Sift dry ingredients together. Add beaten egg, vanilla, and milk. Stir until well blended. Add oil, honey, and apples. Mix thoroughly. Pour batter into greased, shallow, 9-inch pan. Bake at 350° for 25 min.

CRUSTY CORNBREAD

1 c. oat or whole wheat flour	2 c. buttermilk
1 1/2 c. cornmeal	1/2 t. baking soda
2 t. baking powder	1/2 t. salt
1/2 c. sour cream	2 eggs

Preheat oven to 400°. Sift dry ingredients. Make a well in flour and put in eggs, cream, and buttermilk. Stir quickly and pour into a hot, greased, 10 in. frying pan. Bake at 400° until done, 15 to 20 min. Serve immediately with fresh butter and sorghum.

GLUTEN-FREE CORNBREAD▾

1 c. cornmeal	2 t. baking powder
1 c. brown rice flour	1 T. carob powder (optional)
1/4 c. millet or soy flour	1/4 c. canola oil
1 1/2 c. any flavor soy milk	2 eggs

(if whey or yogurt is used, use 1 t. soda instead of baking powder)

Mix all dry ingredients. Add rest of ingredients and mix thoroughly. Pour into greased 9" x 9" pan. Bake at 300° for 45 min to 1 hr. Delicious with butter served warm or with soy milk and/or fruit.

CORN BREAD

1 1/2 c. corn meal	1 egg
3 t. baking powder	1/2 c. oat flour
1 c. milk	1/3 c. honey

Mix well and add 1/4 c. butter melted in a pan you can then use to bake corn bread.

CORN BREAD▾

1 1/2 c. whole grain cornmeal	1 t. salt
1/2 c. whole wheat flour	1/2 t. baking soda
1/4 c. oil	2 eggs
2 t. baking powder	1 1/2 c. water

Bake at 400° in a greased 8" x 8" pan for 25 to 30 min. For cornsticks or muffins, bake 12 to 15 min. Very good, fast and easy.

Variation: Add grated carrots, chopped pecans, grated zucchini, or raisins.

BREADS

BREADS

Oat bran tends to make a moist bread, and care should be taken to avoid underbaking.

CORN BREAD

1 1/2 c. wheat flour	1/4 to 1/2 c. honey or sorghum
1 1/4 c. cornmeal	4 t. baking powder
Mix together and then add:	
2 eggs	a dash of vanilla
3 T. melted butter or oil	

Add enough milk to make the right consistency, like a thick cake batter. If you like it coarse, use more corn meal and less flour. Bake in a slow oven until done.

CORN PONE

1 pt. corn meal	2 pts. whole wheat flour
1/2 c. butter	1 egg
1/3 c. maple syrup	1 t. baking soda
2 t. baking powder	3 c. buttermilk
1 t. salt	

Bake 1/2 hour at 350°.

SPOON BREAD▼

1 1/2 c. water or soy milk	3 eggs, separated
3/4 c. stoneground cornmeal	3 T. cold pressed vegetable oil
3/4 t. (or more) sea salt	

Bring water or milk to boil. Pour in cornmeal, stirring constantly, cooking until thickened. Add salt and lightly beaten eggs yolks and oil. Remove from heat and cool slightly. Fold in stiffly beaten egg whites. Bake in greased 8 in. square baking dish at 375° for 35 to 40 min. Cut in 9 squares.

CREAM PUFFS

1/2 c. butter
1/4 t. salt
1 c. boiling water
4 eggs
1 c. wheat flour

1. Melt butter in boiling water.

2. Add flour and salt at the same time, stirring vigorously. Cool, stirring constantly, until the mixture forms a ball that doesn't separate.

3. Add eggs one at a time, beating hard after each addition, until mixture is smooth.

4. Form cream puffs 2 1/2" in diameter and place 2" apart on greased cookie sheets. Bake until no beads of moisture appear on the cream puffs, and until cream puffs do not fall when taken from the oven.

5. Loosen from sheet.

6. We eat these hot for breakfast with a hot raspberry sauce. Any other berry sauce would work, too.

SOURDOUGH STARTER

2 c. whole wheat flour
2 c. warm water
1 pkg. yeast

Thoroughly blend in large bowl. Leave uncovered in warm spot 48 hours. Stir occasionally. Just before using, take out amount needed. Replenish by blending in 1 c. flour and 1 c. warm water. Leave starter uncovered in warm spot several hours. When it bubbles once more, put in a non-metal container. Cover loosely and store in refrigerator. The night before using again, take out of fridge to warm and commence working. Must be used at least once in 2 weeks. Daily use is best.

BREADS

22

NOTES

breakfasts

BREAKFASTS

Store bought cereals are made with refined grains and have a lot of sugar and additives. One nutritionist said, "We'd be better off eating the box and throwing the cereal away."

WHEAT MUSH

Bring water to a boil. Add a little salt and sprinkle in whole wheat flour until you have the desired consistency.

Variation: Oatmeal, bran, or raisins may be added. Boil a few minutes. Serve hot with milk and sweetener.

QUICK FRIED MUSH▾

4 c. cornmeal	6 c. boiling water
2 t. salt	4 T. flour

Mix dry ingredients. Add water and stir until well mixed. Drop by spoonfuls onto hot skillet. Press flat with spatula. It will brown fast. If batter gets too stiff, add a little more water to make it the consistency you want. Serves a family of eight.

Note: Sprinkle a little flour on your mush in the skillet. Turn around and sprinkle the other side. It will fry faster.

We like to use this to thicken soups instead of store-bough crackers.

CORNMEAL WAFFLES▾

1 c. whole wheat flour	1 1/2 c. yellow cornmeal
2 t. baking powder	2 eggs
1 t. baking soda	1/3 c. oil
3/4 t. salt	1 1/2 c. water (may need more)

Combine ingredients. Beat until smooth. Bake in waffle iron.

BUTTERMILK PANCAKES

2 1/4 c. wheat flour
1 1/2 t. baking powder
1/4 t. cinnamon (optional)
1/2 c. honey
1 to 1 1/4 c. buttermilk or sour milk

1/2 t. salt
4 T. oil
1 t. baking soda
3 eggs

Combine all ingredients, adding buttermilk to make the consistency you desire. Pour by 1/4 cupfuls onto hot griddle or skillet.

CORN MUSH

3 c. corn meal
1 t. salt

1/2 c. whole wheat flour

Moisten with cold water and 1/2 c. milk. Slowly add boiling water; stir until smooth and it starts to boil. It takes 2 1/2 qts. or more of boiling water. Cook 20 minutes. Stir occasionally while cooking.

This is good to eat like a warm cereal with honey and milk. What is left over can be poured into a pan and set in a cold place. Then slice, fry, and eat with syrup.

CORNMEAL MUSH

Heat to boiling 3 c. water.
Mix:
1 c. cold water
1 c. cornmeal

1 t. salt

Add cornmeal mixture into boiling water, stirring constantly. Cook until thickened, stirring frequently. Then cover and cook another 15 minutes over low heat. Pour into loaf pan. When cold, cut into 1/4" thick slices and fry until golden brown. Serve hot with maple syrup or honey.

Corn Meal – Place dry ears of corn on oven rack and turn oven low for a day or overnight. Shell corn and pour from pail to pail 6 to 8 times in a strong wind until corn is cleaned. Grind. (Roasting it in the oven gives an added flavor.)

BREAKFASTS

Add wheat germ to cooked cereals. Vanilla is good in oatmeal.

WAFFLES▾

Separate 3 eggs and whip whites. In another bowl, combine:

1 1/4 c. wheat flour	1 1/2 c. water
4 t. baking powder	egg yolks
1/2 t. salt	1/3 c. oil

OATMEAL PANCAKES

1/2 c. oatmeal	3 t. baking powder
4 T. cornmeal	1 t. salt

enough wheat flour to make 2 c. mix

2 eggs, separated	4 T. melted butter
1 3/4 to 2 c. milk	2 t. honey

Beat egg whites and fold into batter.

OATMEAL PANCAKES▾

2 1/4 c. oatmeal	3 c. buttermilk
1/4 c. cornmeal	1/2 c. whole wheat flour
1 1/2 t. baking soda	1 1/2 t. salt
3 eggs	

OATMEAL BUCKWHEAT PANCAKES

1/2 c. oatmeal	3 t. baking powder
4 T. cornmeal	1 t. salt

1/2 c. buckwheat flour - add enough wheat flour to make 2 c. mix

In separate bowl combine:

2 egg yolks	4 T. oil
1 3/4 c. water	2 t. honey

Now add ingredients from first mix. Next beat egg whites until stiff and fold in batter with wire whip. Pour on hot buttered griddle. Flfuffy and light! Serve with warm maple syrup.

BRAN CAKES

In a bowl, combine:

1/3 c. wheat flour	1/4 t. salt
1/3 c. bran	1 t. oil
1 c. milk or water	1 egg
2 t. baking powder	

Fry as you would regular pancakes. If you would like a denser texture, put in an extra egg.

Variation: Put in sunflower seeds for a tasty addition.

Note: 2 T. bran cake batter will swell up to a 6 inch cake. The oil in the mixture keeps the cakes from sticking and helps hold them together.

WHOLE GRAIN PANCAKES▼

1 c. whole wheat pastry flour	1 3/4 to 2 c. buttermilk or soy milk
3/4 c. brown rice flour	2 eggs
3/4 to 1 c. rolled oats	1/4 c. oil
1 t. baking soda	

Preheat griddle. Mix all dry ingredients. Beat eggs well. Add eggs and remaining ingredients to dry mixture, mixing only until blended. Put oil, the size of a quarter, on griddle, spreading it with a paper towel over the whole griddle. You should not have to add more oil on griddle during baking.

Raisins, chopped dates, or unsweetened coconut added to cereal after cooking make it sweet – naturally.

OLD FASHIONED BUCKWHEAT PANCAKES

1 T. dry yeast
2 1/2 c. warm water
1 c. wheat flour
1 c. buckwheat flour

1 1/2 t. salt
1/4 c. melted btter
1 T. molasses

   Dissolve yeast in warm water. Add flours and salt and beat vigorously until smooth. Cover and refrigerate overnight. In the morning, stir in the butter and molasses. Let stand at room temperature for 30 minutes. Bake on hot grill. Makes 36 pancakes.

BUCKWHEAT PANCAKES▼

1 1/2 to 2 c. buckwheat flour
1 1/2 c. water
3 T. sesame or other oil
2 fresh eggs
1 apple or 1/2 c. applesauce (unsweetened)

2 T. apple butter (unsweetened)
1/4 t. cinnamon (optional)
1/4 t. vanilla (optional)

   Blend together all wet ingredients. Mix in the flour. Stir until mixed well and fry.

BUCKWHEAT PANCAKES▾

2 c. buckwheat flour
(1 c. whole wheat pastry flour can be used, or part oatmeal)
2 t. baking powder (or 1 t. baking soda if buttermilk is used)
1 1/2 to 2 c. soy milk, or buttermilk
1/4 c. oil
1 c. unsweetened applesauce or 1/2 c. water

   Mix dry ingredients. Mix wet ingredients. Now combine the two, mixing only until blended. Pour oil the size of a quarter onto griddle. With a paper towel spread oil over the whole griddle. You shouldn't need to add more oil during baking.

   Note: The applesauce makes it more moist.

   Optional: Sesame seeds can be added to any pancake batter.

   Note: For one allergic to yeast breads – use buckwheat pancakes for bread.

CORN MUSH PANCAKES

1 1/2 c. pre-cooked corn mush
3/4 c. whole wheat or oat flour

3 eggs	2 t. baking powder
1/2 t. salt	1 c. milk

   Put all ingredients in a bowl and beat up with a potato masher as cold corn mush is fairly firm. If a thinner dough is desired, add more milk. Bake on moderately hot griddle or frying pan, using butter as needed.

   Note: I use very little butter. These pancakes are very tender and delicious, served with syrup or honey.

Spread apple slices with any nut butter and roll in wheat germ.

BREAKFASTS

Sweeten cereal with fresh fruits, such as bananas or berries.

PANCAKE MIX▼

2 1/2 c. whole wheat flour	1 1/2 c. powdered milk
1 1/2 c. rye flour	1 T. salt
1 c. cornmeal	3 t. baking powder

Mix and store in a cold place in a tight container.

To make pancakes:

1 1/2 c. mix	1 egg
2 T. canola oil	

Add enough water to attain desired consistency.

WHOLE GRAIN PANCAKE MIX

3 c. whole wheat flour	1 c. cornmeal
2 1/2 c. rye or buckwheat flour	5 T. baking powder
1/2 c. oatmeal	1 T. salt
1 c. wheat germ	2 T. lecithin

Mix and store in refrigerator. To make pancakes:

2 c. milk or water	1/2 c. oil
2 eggs	2 c. mix*

Combine milk, eggs, and oil. Add to mix and stir just until mixed. Bake on griddle.

For ginger cakes, add to the above recipe 1 t. each of ginger, cloves, and cinnamon. When baked, top with applesauce.

WAFFLE OR PANCAKE TOPPINGS▼

1. Thin peanut butter with water. Add a little cinnamon, or if you may use fruit, add a mashed banana.

2. Save leftover juice from peaches, pears, or whatever you have that has been canned without sweetener. Thicken slightly with tapioca starch. Serve warm.

GRAPENUTS

6 c. rye or wheat flour
3 c. oat flour or oats
3 c. cornmeal
1/2 c. cane molasses
1 c. honey

1 pt. cream
1 pt. buttermilk
4 t. baking soda
2 t. salt
2 t. maple flavoring

Bake in moderate oven. Put through 1/4 inch screen while warm, then toast in oven.

GRAPENUTS

6 cups graham flour
1 t. salt
1 t. vanilla
1 t. maple flavoring
1 t. cinnamon

1/4 c. oil or melted butter
1/2 c. honey
2 t. baking soda
2 1/2 to 3 c. milk or buttermilk

Mix baking soda with milk. Mix oil and honey together. Now mix these two mixtures with the rest of the ingredients. Pour into a 9" x 13" cake pan and bake at 350° for 35 to 40 minutes. Let cool, then crumble up and put on cookie sheets. Best when only a layer or so in the pan at a time. Toast at 250° until slightly browned.

BUTTERMILK GRAPENUTS

10 1/2 c. whole wheat flour
5 to 6 c. buttermilk
1/2 c. cane molasses
3 t. salt

2 c. maple syrup
1/2 c. honey
3 t. baking soda

Mix well. Pour into two buttered cake pans. Bake at 300° for 1 1/2 hr.

BREAKFASTS

Sesame seeds give cereal and desserts a nutty flavor.

ZUCCHINI PANCAKES

3 c. wheat flour	1/2 t. salt
2 t. baking powder	2 T. oil
1 c. grated zucchini	2 1/2 c. milk
1 c. grated cheese	2 eggs, separated

Mix dry ingredients, then add other ingredients. Last, fold in stiffly beaten egg whites. Fry in lightly oiled or buttered skillet.

Note: These pancakes are good with gravy or applesauce.

FRUIT SYRUP

1 qt. unsweetened fruit juice   1 T. honey or maple syrup

Bring to a boil and thicken with cornstarch. Serve hot or cold over pancakes or French toast.

Note: If you wish to be economical, use leftover canned peach or pear juice.

CIDER SNITZ (UNSWEETENED)▾

For topping for pancakes instead of syrup or apple butter, etc., cook dried snitz in canned apple juice or cider. Add spices and lemon juice or a little Powdered C (Neo Life product) to suit taste. Add apple juice until you have the desired thickness. This is very delicious with pancakes and eggs.

CHEESE SOUFFLE

8 slices of bread
1 lb. grated cheese
6 beaten eggs
1 small finely chopped onion

mushrooms (or meat of your choice)
seasonings to taste
2 c. milk
1/4 c. butter

Cube bread and put in bottom of casserole. Combine cheese, butter, and mushrooms. Sprinkle over bread cubes. Mix egg, milk, onion, and seasonings. Pour over other ingredients. Refrigerate overnight. Bake at 325° for 45 minutes.

This is a very handy dish when you have overnight guests for breakfast.

SCRAMBLED EGGS

When scrambling eggs, you may wish to add cheese, some milk, green peppers, onions, mushrooms, etc.

SCRAPPLE

Boil 2 qts. water or broth with 2 t. salt. Slowly add 1 c. whole millet. Cook slowly until millet is nearly soft. Then add 1 c. cornmeal, 1/2 c. wheat flour moistened in cold water, and 1 pt. ground meat or liver. Turn heat on low and cook 1/2 to 1 hr. Pour into loaf pans and cool. Slice to fry.

EGG DUTCH

5 eggs
1/3 c. wheat flour
1 t. Vege-sal

dash of pepper
1/4 t. baking powder
2 c. milk

Combine all ingredients in a mixing bowl. Pour into hot, greased skillet on medium-low heat. Turn with scraper now and then, until egg dutch is all set. Serve immediately. Serves 4 to 6.

OMELET

6 potatoes
12 eggs
1 c. milk

1/4 t. salt
cheese

Shoestring potatoes and fry until tender. Beat eggs, milk, and salt, and pour over potatoes. Cover pan until the eggs are ready to turn. Turn and put slices of cheese on top. Cover again until cheese is melted. Serves 8.

SOFT BOILED EGGS

Soft boiling eggs for breakfast is much healthier than frying them. Bring your water to a boil. Place your eggs in the water and begin timing immediately. When eggs are at room temperature, boil for 3 minutes. If they are colder, it will take longer. Experiment until you know how much time it takes for the consistency you want. The less they are heated, the better, of course. Nutritional yeast from the health food store sprinkled onto the eggs is good.

BREAKFAST YOGURT

1 c. yogurt
3 dates, sliced
1/4 red apple, diced
1/2 small banana, sliced

1 T. chopped nuts
honey or maple syrup to taste
1/4 c. granola

Spoon yogurt into breakfast bowl and top with remaining ingredients, reserving honey to pour on top. Enjoy! 1 serving.

FRIED OAT CEREAL

1/2 c. oil
3 1/2 c. quick oats
1/2 c. coconut
1/2 c. pecans

vanilla to taste
1/2 c. honey
3/4 c. wheat germ

Heat oil in frying pan and add oatmeal. Turn heat to simmer and add other ingredients. Last, add wheat germ and honey, heating until it is as crisp and brown as you desire (about 1 minute).

BEST GRANOLA

5 c. oatmeal
1 1/2 c. coconut
3/4 c. wheat germ
3/4 c. walnut pieces
1/2 c. melted butter

1 c. maple syrup
1/3 c. sesame seeds
1 t. cinnamon
1 t. vanilla

Mix dry ingredients thoroughly. Then mix syrup, butter, and vanilla, and pour over the rest. Bake at 300° to 325° for 30 minutes, stirring frequently.

GRANOLA

6 c. oatmeal
1/2 c. sunflower seeds
1/2 c. sesame seeds
1/3 c. olive oil
1 t. nutmeg

2 c. coconut
1 c. wheat germ
1 c. maple syrup
1 T. orange juice
1 t. almond extract

Mix dry ingredients thoroughly, then mix the rest of the ingredients separately and pour over the first mixture.

Bake at 300° to 325° for 30 minutes, stirring occasionally.

Wheat germ sprinkled onto cooked cereals gives it an added flavor.

When adding raisins to granola, do so after toasting. This will prevent them from hardening.

Raisins, chopped dates, or unsweetened coconut added to cereal after cooking make it sweet naturally.

BAKED OATMEAL

3 c. oatmeal	1 t. salt
1/2 c. sorghum	1 c. rice milk or water
2 t. baking powder	2 eggs, beaten
1 1/2 t. cinnamon	1/2 c. oil or melted butter

Mix all ingredients together. Spoon into greased 9" baking dish. Bake at 350° for 40 to 45 minutes. Serve warm with frozen blueberries, canned fruit or milk. Delicious!

GRANOLA

4 1/2 c. butter	26 c. quick oats
2 3/4 c. honey	28 c. wheat flour
1 1/4 c. cane molasses	2 T. vanilla
3 c. shredded coconut	

Use large dish pan. Melt butter, honey, and molasses together and add remaining ingredients. Brown in moderate oven for around 1 hr. or until lightly browned. Stir often.

GRANOLA▼

10 c. oatmeal	1 c. wheat bran
2 c. wheat germ	1 1/2 c. canola oil
2 c. nuts	1 c. apple juice concentrate or water
2 c. unsweetened coconut	2 T. vanilla
1 c. sesame seeds	1 T. salt
1/2 c. flax seeds	

Heat oil, apple juice, vanilla, and salt. Stir well and pour over dry ingredients that were well mixed. Bake at 250° about 1 hour until crisp. Stir every 15 minutes.

Variation: Can add cinnamon to dry ingredients or 1 t. orange extract and 1 t. coconut extract to liquid.

GRANOLA BREAKFAST CEREAL

7 c. rolled oats	1 c. ground nuts
2 1/2 c. unsweetened shredded coconut	
2 c. wheat germ	1 t. salt
1/2 c. oil	2 t. cinnamon
1/2 c. honey	2 t. vanilla
1 c. raisins	

Put oil in a measuring cup, then add honey and mix. This order is important so it slides out easier. Put all other ingredients, except raisins, in a mixing bowl. Pour oil-honey mixture over it all and mix with hands. Put on cookie sheets and toast in 250° oven for 1/2 to 3/4 hr. More or less, depends on how full you make the cookie sheets. The granola should be just lightly browned and not wet-feeling to the touch. Put raisins in a bowl and dump toasted cereal on top. When cool, mix together with hands. Store in plastic bags or air-tight container.

Variety: Sesame seeds and dried apple bits can also be added.

SPICY UNBAKED GRANOLA

4 3/4 lb. oatmeal	1 t. allspice
3 c. whole wheat flour	1 t. salt
3 c. wheat bran	2 c. ground roasted sunflower seeds
2 c. barley flour	1 3/4 lb. raisins
4 t. cinnamon	

Mix well. Add 2 c. honey and 1/2 c. blackstrap molasses. Work in well with hands. Serve as is.

If your family gets tired of eating the same cooked cereals, try steel cut oats, 7 grain, cracked wheat, or bear mush. Bring water to a boil, add cereal and simmer on low heat until done. Most can be cooked in 10 to 15 minutes.

To make granola chunky, add flour or dry milk, and water along with oil and honey.

PEANUT BUTTER GRANOLA

5 1/2 c. oatmeal	4 T. vegetable oil
1/2 c. wheat germ	1/2 c. honey
1/2 c. oat bran	1 t. vanilla
1 c. raisins	2/3 c. peanut butter

Mix first three ingredients. Heat oil and honey in a saucepan over low heat. Remove, add vanilla and peanut butter while warm. Combine with dry ingredients. Pour on cookie sheet and bake at 225° until golden brown. Stir frequently. Add raisins after granola is cooled so they do not harden.

3-GRAIN CEREAL

Mix, beating well:

1/2 c. shortening	1 c. honey
2 eggs	

Add:

1 t. salt	2 c. whole wheat flour
3 t. baking powder	1 c. cornmeal
1 1/2 c. milk, sweet or sour	

Mix well and bake in loaf pan for 40 minutes at 325°. The thinner the dough, the higher it will rise, especially if baked in glass pan.

When baked, cut cake into small, 3/8 to 1/2 inch squares.

Add 2 c. oatmeal and 1 c. wheat germ. Toast in oven, stirring occasionally, until squares are crunchy. Remove from oven and add 1 c. dried apples, 1 c. raisins, and 1 c. coconut. (These last ingredients are optional.) The cake is good served with milk, also.

main dishes

4-LAYER MEAL

1 lb. hamburger
2 c. cooked corn
2 c. grated raw potatoes

salt and pepper to taste
cheese to melt

Fry and season hamburger until done in a skillet. Spread grated potatoes on top of hamburger. Salt and pepper to taste, then spread on corn. Sprinkle on a little salt. Last, arrange slices of cheese on top of corn. Cover and turn really low for 20 minutes or until it looks bubbly. Serves 4 to 6.

BUSY MOTHER CASSEROLE▾

1 1/2 lb. ground turkey
1 egg
1/4 t. garlic salt
dash of red pepper

1 carrot or more
1 medium onion
6 medium-sized potatoes
1 t. salt

1 head broccoli or green beans (fresh or frozen)

Season turkey and egg with salt, garlic salt, and red pepper. Mix well and put in bottom of 6 or 8 qt. casserole dish. Next, put broccoli and carrots, and then a thin layer of onions. Spread thinly sliced potatoes on top. Sprinkle a little salt on potatoes. Cover and bake at 325° for 1 to 1 1/2 hrs. Deliciously simple – a one-dish meal.

EASY BEAN AND LENTIL CASSEROLE

4 c. water
4 med. carrots, sliced in circles
1/2 c. adjuki beans

1/2 c. lentils
1 c. brown rice
Vege-sal to taste

Place carrots and water in casserole. Add rest of ingredients. Bake at 350° for 1 1/2 to 2 hrs. Yummy!

FARMER'S DELIGHT CASSEROLE

5 peeling size potatoes (can be cooked)
1 qt. canned green beans
1 lb. hamburger, fried   3 T. whole wheat flour
2 T. butter   salt and pepper to taste

   In skillet, melt butter. Add flour and brown for a few minutes, stirring with a fork, so it doesn't burn. Add liquid, a little at a time, stirring constantly, until it is the consistency of a white sauce. Green bean juice, milk, sour cream, buttermilk, or a combination may be used for the liquid. Season to taste. I like to add a little cheese, soy sauce, and garlic or onion salt.

   Cut potatoes into bite size pieces. Mix potatoes, green beans, hamburger, and sauce. Pour into a casserole dish. If potatoes are cooked, bake for 30 min. If potatoes are not cooked, bake for 1 hr.

   Note: The last 10 min. cheese and bread crumbs can be put on top if you wish.

EL RANCHO CASSEROLE

2 lbs. ground turkey   1 t. chili powder
1 onion, chopped   1 t. salt
3/4 c. macaroni (from health food store)
1 can tomatoes   1/4 t. pepper

   Brown meat and onion. Add the rest of the ingredients and simmer, covered, until macaroni is done.

Try to avoid using a pressure cooker. High heat and high pressure destroys nutrients. Steaming vegetable or cooking waterless is the best way.

MAIN DISHES

Since boiled potatoes turn out mushy when defrosted, they do not freeze well. But you can freeze potatoes if you bake them first. They keep a much nicer texture and can be used in cooked dishes such as stews, soups and casseroles.

DINNER IN A DISH▼

1 medium onion, chopped	2 eggs
2 green peppers, chopped	4 medium tomatoes
1 lb. ground turkey	1/4 t. pepper
1 1/2 t. salt	2 c. corn

Fry onion and peppers and brown the meat. Add salt and pepper and toss in eggs. Mix well. Put half the corn in an 8" x 8" baking dish. Layer meat, tomatoes, and corn, etc. Bake at 375° for 35 min.

ONE DISH MEAL

1 lb. hamburger	1 onion, chopped
1 c. cooked rice	1 c. olives
1/4 c. chopped, green pepper	2 c. undiluted tomato soup
1/2 lb. cheese	1 c. mushrooms

Sauté hamburger, peppers, and onion. Add rest of ingredients. Bake in loaf pan at 300° for 1 1/2 hrs. Serves 5.

SKILLET MEAL▼

Brown 1 lb. ground turkey in skillet. Sprinkle with seasonings. Layer vegetables in order and sprinkle with salt. Use these vegetables or whatever is in season:

potatoes	new green beans
onions	peas
carrots	asparagus
celery	young squash

Last, top with a can of tomatoes and a little of the juice. Put on the lid and cook fast for 10 min. or until tender.

TURKEY POT PIE

1 c. chopped onions	parsley for garnish
1 c. chopped celery	1/2 c. wheat flour
1 c. chopped carrots	2 c. turkey broth
1/2 c. chopped sweet pepper	1 c. light cream
1/3 c. melted butter	2 t. salt
4 c. chopped, cooked turkey	1/4 t. pepper
biscuit or basic pastry dough	

Preheat oven to 400°. Sauté vegetables in butter for 10 min. Add flour to sautéed vegetables, cook 1 min., stirring constantly. Combine broth and light cream. Gradually stir into vegetable mixture, stirring constantly, until thickened and bubbly. Stir in salt and pepper. Add meat, stirring well. Pour mixture into 2 qt. casserole dish. Top with layer of biscuit or basic pastry dough. Cut slits to allow steam to escape. Bake 40 min. Garnish with parsley.

Note: If using seasoning salt, use only 1 t. salt. Chicken may be used instead of turkey.

DELICIOUS CABBAGE STEW▾

Fill a 2 qt. saucepan 1/2 full of water or vegetable broth. Heat to boiling, then add:

1/4 head of cabbage, cut up fine

1 or 2 medium-sized potatoes, cubed

1 small onion	
1 large carrot, grated coarsely	1 t. soy sauce
1 or 2 stalks celery, chopped	Vege-sal to taste
	1 t. or more butter

Simmer on low heat. Wait to add celery, carrots, onion, and soy sauce until potatoes and cabbage are about 1/2 done. Add all but butter and simmer a few minutes longer. Do not overcook. Add butter before serving. Serves 4 to 6.

Use cooked rice with Parsley Patch seasoning and a little Veg-sal or salt, adding some rich broth from roasting chicken. Also add soy milk and soy sauce. It is delicious served with roasted chicken and vegetables.

Add wheat germ to cooked cereals. Vanilla is also good in oatmeal.

GRATED POTATO CASSEROLE

8 or 9 medium potatoes, cooked in skin, peeled and grated
  Melt:

2 T. butter	3/4 c. Colby cheese
1 t. salt	1/2 c. sour cream
1 1/2 c. milk	

  Using a greased casserole dish, alternately layer potatoes and cheese mixture until all are used. Sprinkle top with whole wheat bread crumbs. Bake uncovered for 1 hr. at 350°.

NO NAME CASSEROLE

1 1/4 lb. hamburger, browned	1 can tomato soup
1 onion	1 can water
1 green pepper	1 T. chili powder
1 c. whole kernel corn, drained	

  Combine and place in large casserole dish. Cover casserole with bread crumbs. Bake at 375° until browned and done.

SPRING PEAS AND POTATOES

  Wash and cook small, new potatoes, and slice them into bottom of casserole dish. Top with fresh, cooked peas, and cover with plenty of white sauce. Shred cheese on top and bake just until cheese is melted.

THREE SISTERS CASSEROLE

3 c. shredded zucchini	1 onion, chopped
3/4 lb. hamburger	2 c. cooked lima beans
2 medium tomatoes, chopped	1/2 t. sage or thyme
1/4 c. shopped, fresh parsley	1 1/2 t. salt
1 1/2 c. cooked corn	1/8 t. pepper
1 slice wheat bread, crumbled	Cheese sauce (recipe follows)

In medium skillet, brown hamburger and onion. Stir in chopped tomatoes, parsley, salt, sage, and pepper. Bring to a boil and reduce heat. Cover and simmer 5 minutes. Remove from heat. Stir in bread crumbs, beans, and corn. Set aside. Prepare cheese sauce. Layer half the zucchini in a casserole dish. Spread half the meat mixture on top, then 1/2 of the sauce. Repeat layers, ending with sauce. Sprinkle with cheese if desire.

Cheese sauce:

In saucepan, melt 3 T. butter. Stir in 2 c. milk. Slowly stir in 2 heaping T. wheat flour, 1/2 t. salt, and 1 t. soy sauce. Cook, stirring constantly, until mixture thickens and boils. Remove from heat. Stir in 1 heaping T. yogurt or sour cream. Stir in 3/4 c. cheese chunks.

HAY STACKS

1/2 head lettuce, cut up	2 c. croutons
1 large carrot, grated fine	1 c. salad dressing
4 hard boiled eggs, grated	(Sweet-n-Sour works well)
2 c. brown rice, cooked and cooled	Salsa, optional

Mix the eggs, carrots and lettuce. Serve the rice and croutons in separate bowls.

To eat put a serving of the lettuce mixture on plate, top with rice and salad dressing. Toss on croutons. Delicious! This recipe could be varied by adding tomatoes, leftover baked beans, sour cream or hot taco sauce.

MAIN DISHES

Pre-cooked rice is good with almost any vegetable or mixed vegetables. Add soy sauce, soy milk or chicken broth.

BROWN RICE WITH ZUCCHINI SAUCE▾

Prepare the rice:

2 c. brown rice	1 - 2 T. unrefined safflower oil
4 c. water	1 t. sea salt

Measure the rice into a large saucepan with a tight-fitting lid. Add the water, oil, and salt. Bring to a boil and stir briefly. Cover tightly and simmer 17 min. over low heat. Remove the lid. Fluff the rice with a fork.

Prepare the zucchini sauce:

3 T. unrefined oil	1 t. Indo
3 lbs. fresh zucchini, small variety	1 c. water
1 t. oregano	

Heat the oil in a heavy saucepan. Coarsely chop the zucchini and add it to the oil. Sauté it momentarily, stirring well to coat with oil. Add the oregano, Indo, and water. Bring to boil, stirring constantly. Reduce the heat and simmer, tightly covered, for 5 to 10 min., or until the zucchini is tender and forms a rich sauce. Spoon over bowls of hot rice. Serves 4.

BAKED RICE▾

1 1/2 c. cooked brown rice	2 T. each of the following:
2 c. chicken broth	minced celery
1 c. hot water	minced onion
1 t. salt	minced pepper
1/4 t. garlic powder	oil
1/8 t. pepper	1 t. parsley

Mix in greased 1 1/2 qt. casserole dish. Cover and bake at 350° for 1 hr.

DELICIOUS FRIED BROWN RICE

1 1/2 c. brown rice	2 qts. water
2 c. hamburger	1 onion
2 c. pizza sauce	salt and pepper to taste

Cook brown rice in water for 40 min. or until tender. Fry onion and hamburger together, then add the pizza sauce. Stir in cooked rice and salt and pepper to taste.

FRIED RICE▾

Sauté 1 chopped onion in oil. Add 1 1/2 c. brown rice. Cook over medium heat, stirring constantly until rice is golden. Add 2 c. plus 3 T. water. Cover. Simmer 45 minutes or until rice is tender. Add more water if necessary.

RICE/LEGUME CASSEROLE▾

2/3 to 3/4 c. brown rice	1 t. soy sauce
1/2 c. split peas or part lentils	some chopped carrots are good also
1 small onion	3 c. water (or part milk or soy milk)
seasoning to taste	

You may have to add more liquid before serving.

Mix all ingredients and place in a 2 qt. casserole dish. Bake at 350° for 1 1/2 hrs.

Note: This recipe can be varied a lot. Use your imagination with vegetables. For fresh vegetables, add the last 1/2 hr. or so. You may also include chicken and broth if you wish.

To cook brown rice or millet, soak several hours in water before heating. Then simmer slowly until soft. This method preserves taste and vitamin content.

BROWN RICE AND CHICKEN▾

1 c. brown rice
1 small onion
Vege-sal and soy sauce to taste
3 to 4 c. liquid (part water, part milk, or soy milk may be used)
2 c. deboned chicken and broth
   Combine and bake at 350° for 1 1/2 hrs. Chicken may be thickened like gravy and added to rice after it is baked.

CHICKEN AND RICE▾

   Fry in oil:
1 medium onion   1 green pepper, chopped
   Add to 3 1/2 c. chicken broth.
   Add 1 t. oregano, 2 bay leaves, and 1 1/2 t. salt. Bring to a boil. Add 1 1/2 c. brown rice. Pour into casserole and add 2 c. chopped chicken. Bake at 300° for 1 1/2 hrs. or until rice is soft.
   Note: This is delicious served with green peas.

PERFECT BROWN RICE▾

1 c. brown rice (long, medium, or short grain)
2 1/2 c. water
1 t. sea salt
1 T. unrefined safflower oil
   Place all the ingredients in a saucepan with a tight-fitting lid, in the order given. Bring to a boil and stir gently with a fork. Cover and simmer over low heat for 40 min. Do not lift the lid while rice is cooking. Remove from heat and allow to stand 10 to 20 min. with the lid on before serving. Serves 2.

SESAME RICE▾

1 c. onions, chopped	1/8 t. garlic powder
1 3/4 c. brown rice	2 T. sesame seeds
2 T. parsley	

Stir altogether in a large, hot, dry skillet. Stir-fry about 10 min. until rice is brown and popping.

Pour 3 c. water over the rice. Cover and simmer for 20 min. Stir in 1/2 t. salt. Cover and simmer another 15 min. Stir in 3 T. Nutritional Yeast. Serve.

Suggestion: Serve with butternut squash rolls and carrot sticks.

Variation: Add 1 t. curry powder when salt is added.

RICE CASSEROLE

1 onion, chopped fine	2 1/2 T. whole wheat flour
4 c. cooked brown rice	bread crumbs or bran or crackers
1/2 c. cheese	1 beaten egg

Bake at 350° for 1/2 hour.

CHOP SUEY

4 c. rice	1 c. diced celery

Cook together.

2 T. oil	2 onions
1 lb. hamburger	

Fry onions in oil and add hamburger. When hamburger is fried, add ingredients for sauce:

1 T. soy sauce (optional)	1 c. mushrooms (optional)
2 T. cornstarch	1/2 t. salt
2 T. molasses	

Mix, then pour over cooked rice and celery. Simmer for 15 min.

When adding herbs for flavor, do so after it is cooked, but still hot and let stand 10 minutes. If added before, it will lead to overcooking of the herbs and you will lose the flavor. Sometimes it even draws out a bitter taste.

FAMILY FAVORITE ZUCCHINI

3 eggs

3/4 c. honey

1 c. oil

2 c. raw, grated zucchini

1 c. bran

1 c. chopped dates

1 c. chopped nuts (optional)

2 c. flour - barley

1 t. baking soda

1/2 t. baking powder

orange flavoring

   Sift flour, baking powder, and baking soda. Beat eggs well and add oil, honey, and flavoring. Carefully fold in zucchini last. Bake at 350° for 35 min. or until golden brown.

ZUCCHINI VEGETABLE DISH

6 c. zucchini or squash

3 medium tomatoes

2 c. diced carrots

2 T. butter

1 T. basil

1 chopped onion

2 c. peas

2 c. string beans

seasonings

   Put in casserole dish and bake for 1 1/2 hours. Top with cheese or bread crumbs.

ZUCCHINI STICKS

1/2 c. cornmeal

1/2 c. grated Colby cheese

3 small zucchini, peeled

homemade salad dressing or mayonnaise

   Heat oven to 425°.

   Combine cornmeal and cheese. Set aside. Slice zucchini into sticks. Dip or spread each slice with mayonnaise and roll in cornmeal mixture. Arrange on greased cookie sheet. Bake 15 min., then turn and bake 5 min. more. Serve warm.

ZUCCHINI HAMBURGER BAKE

1 lb. ground hamburger	2 - 3 medium zucchini, grated
1/4 t. onion salt	Colby cheese
1/2 c. bread crumbs	1 c. sour cream
salt and pepper to taste	

Heat oven to 350°. Cook hamburger until completely done. Stir in onion salt, bread crumbs, 2 slices of Colby cheese, and sour cream. Set aside. Sprinkle salt and pepper to taste on zucchini. Put half the zucchini in a 2 qt. casserole dish. Spread hamburger mixture evenly on top and cover with remaining zucchini. Cover and bake 35 min. Uncover and arrange slices of Colby cheese on top. Bake uncovered 10 min. longer until cheese is nicely melted.

A few drops of lemon juice added to simmering rice will keep the grains separate.

ZUCCHINI CASSEROLE

3 c. grated zucchini	1 c. wheat flour
1/2 c. chopped onion	4 eggs
3 t. baking powder	1/2 c. cheese
garlic and parsley salt	1 t. salt

Mix all ingredients together and pour into a casserole dish. Bake at 350° for 35 min.

ZUCCHINI FRITTERS▾

2 c. shredded zucchini	1/2 c. flour
2 eggs, separated	salt to taste

Mix beaten egg yolks with zucchini. Add flour. Fold in stiffly beaten egg whites. Drop like patties into skillet and fry.

MAIN DISHES

Cook vegetables without salt and serve plain. To give them flavor, add parsley or garlic to potatoes; celery seed, onion, or nutmeg to peas; cinnamon, nutmeg or cloves to carrots; and green pepper or onion to corn.

OKRA AND TOMATOES▼

4 slices toasted bread (yeast free)
1/4 c. chopped onion
1 or 2 jalapeño peppers, chopped
4 c. sliced okra
3 c. peeled, chopped tomatoes
1 t. salt
1/2 t. pepper

Toast bread and set aside. Sauté onion and pepper until tender. Add remaining ingredients and cook over medium heat 10 min., stirring occasionally. Add crumbled toasted bread crumbs and serve.

BAKED SAUERKRAUT

1 qt. sauerkraut
1 c. finely chopped onions
1/2 c. sorghum molasses

Mix together and put in casserole. Add enough water to ensure it doesn't bake dry. Put in oven at 350° for 1 hr. or more.

BAKED CARROTS

6 carrots, cooked and mashed

Mix 6 T. melted butter, 1/3 c. grated cheese, 1 beaten egg, 1 c. milk, and 1 T. honey. Add carrots.

Pour into buttered baking dish and top with 1/2 c. cracker or bread crumbs. Bake at 350° until done. Serves 6.

CARROT NUT LOAF

2 c. coarsely chopped carrots
1/2 c. toasted bread crumbs
1 c. chopped celery

3/4 c. chopped walnuts
1 c. mashed tomatoes
1/2 c. braised, sliced onions

Mix together. Add 2 T. butter, place in loaf pan, and bake 1 hr.

LENTILBURGERS

2 c. raw lentils
5 c. water
1 c. quick oats
1 small onion

1/2 c. catsup
2 eggs
1 t. garlic powder
whole wheat flour

Bring water and lentils to a boil. Then simmer until lentils have absorbed nearly all the water. Mix lentils together with remaining ingredients. Form into patties, using enough flour so they keep their shape. Broil in oven and serve like hamburgers.

CHICKEN FRITTERS

4 c. chicken, cut up fine
1/2 c. mushrooms
4 c. mashed potatoes

4 eggs
1/2 c. celery, chopped
1 small onion

Cook onion and celery and mix all ingredients together. Add a little soup or milk to moisten. Press into patties and roll in bread or cracker crumbs and fry.

MAIN DISHES

MAIN DISHES

After flouring chicken, chill for one hour. The coating adheres better during frying.

BREAD STUFFING

1/4 c. butter	1/2 t. dried marjoram
1 1/2 c. chopped onion	1/2 t. dried thyme
1 1/2 c. chopped celery	1/2 t. ground celery seed
1 c. grated carrots	freshly ground pepper
12 c. whole grain bread, cubed	salt to taste
2 t. ground sage	onion salt to taste

Stock:

2 T. poultry seasoning	2 beaten eggs
2 T. nutritional yeast	4 1/2 c. cold water

Dissolve seasoning and yeast in cold water. Saute butter, onion, carrots and celery till a little soft. Add cubes, herbs and seasonings. Mix well and cook for 5 minutes. Bring stock to boil and add to first mixture. Mix well and cook covered for 30 minutes, stirring frequently.

DRESSED-UP STEAK

3 lbs. steak	1/4 c. honey
2 T. olive oil	1 T. soy sauce
1 1/2 c. celery	1 t. salt
4 1/2 oz. pineapple chunks	1 large onion, sliced
1 fresh tomato, cubed	1 diced green pepper
1 T. cornstarch	

Brown meat in oil and remove. Sauté onion, celery, and pepper in oil for about 5 minutes. Drain pineapple and add the chunks and tomato to the vegetables. Moisten cornstarch with pineapple juice (1/2 c.); add honey and sauce. Blend into vegetables; add meat. Cover and cook at 325° for 2 hours or until tender. Stir occasionally to prevent sticking. Serves 6.

MOM'S MEAT LOAF

3 lbs. hamburger
2 eggs
3/4 c. oatmeal
1/4 c. milk
  Topping:
1/2 c. catsup
1/4 c. honey

1 small onion, chopped fine
pinch of salt
pinch of garlic powder
pinch of onion powder

1 t. mustard

Mix in order given and bake in 350° oven for 3/4 hour, then put on the topping and bake until done.

EGGPLANT PATTIES

3 medium eggplant
3/4 c. wheat flour
1 c. quick oats
pepper to taste
garlic powder to taste

2 eggs
1 t. salt
1/2 t. sage
2 T. honey

Peel eggplant and cut into chunks. Cook until soft. You should have about 2 1/2 c. of pulp. Mash pulp and combine with the rest of the ingredients. Drop by tablespoonfuls into a frying pan or skillet. Fry on both sides until browned. Can be served with apple butter, catsup, or honey.

A little baking powder added to meat loaf will make it more fluffy, and if you add 1/2 c. milk to a pound of hamburger and let it set for 1 to 1 1/2 hours before baking, it will be more juicy.

MAIN DISHES

If your baked beans seem to be drying out while baking them, put slices of bread on top of beans. Discard bread before serving beans.

BAKED BEANS

Soak 1 lb. dried beans overnight and cook until soft. Drain off all water. Add:

1 1/2 c. sorghum	1 1/4 t. salt
1/2 c. catsup	pinch of baking soda
2 c. tomato juice	1 T. mustard
2 T. vinegar	
2 c. hamburger (or meat of your choice)	

Mix. Bake 1 hr. in moderately hot oven.

BAKED BEANS

4 c. cooked baby lima beans	1 T. tamari or soy sauce
1 c. water or cooking liquid from beans	
1/2 c. tomato sauce	2 cloves garlic
2 T. chopped onions	1 orange, thinly sliced

Put the lima beans in a 1 1/2 qt. casserole. Blend the water with the tomato sauce, onions, and tamari. Push the garlic through a garlic press into the mixture. Pour over beans and stir lightly. Top with the orange slices. Cover and bake at 350° for 1 hour. Uncover and bake an additional 1 hour. Serves 8.

BOSTON BAKED BEANS

2 c. beans (equal parts of kidney, pinto and navy is a good mix)

Soak overnight, drain, cover with 1" fresh water. Cook till almost tender, about 1 hour on low to medium heat. Drain off the bean broth, then add the following:

1/3 c. sorghum	3/4 c. onion, chopped
1 t. honey	1/4 t. garlic salt
3/4 T. salt	4 T. oil

Return enough of the broth to the beans to give them a sauce. Bake in a covered dish for 1 hour at 350°.

BARBECUE LENTILS

Simmer 25 minutes:

4 c. water	1 1/2 c. lentils
1/2 t. salt	1/8 t. garlic salt
1 c. water	1/2 c. rice
1 bay leaf	

Add to above and simmer 5 minutes:

1 c. chopped onion	4 grated carrots

Add to above and simmer 10 minutes uncovered:

1/4 t. thyme	1 T. parsley
1/2 t. ginger	1/8 t. cloves
1/4 c. honey	1/4 c. vinegar
1/2 T. blackstrap molasses	

TVP BURGERS

1 c. TVP granules	1/2 t. fennel seed (can use ground)
1 c. boiling water	1 t. oregano
1 t. sage	1/2 t. salt
1/8 t. nutmeg	1/2 t. garlic powder
1/8 t. allspice	1/4 c. whole wheat flour
1/2 t. dry mustard	Pizza sauce
1/8 t. cayenne pepper (optional)	

Combine TVP and boiling water in a medium bowl; let stand 5 minutes. Add remaining ingredients except pizza sauce and mix well. Form mixture into patties, brown both sides on a buttered skillet. Place a generous amount of pizza sauce in a casserole dish, then add patties. Continue layering burgers with sauce on each one and enough to cover the tops of the last ones. Bake for 30 minutes at 350°. Serve on buns.

MAIN DISHES

TVP is a textured vegetable protein available at natural food stores. An inexpensive protein alternative that cooks up deliciously! When using, always rehydrate with an equal amount of boiling water for 5 minutes.

MAIN DISHES

Some brands of salt have dextrose in them, which is a sugar. Use sea salt, Indo, or Spike, which can be bought at health food stores. Indo and Spike are made of dried vegetables and spices.

HAMBURGER CUPCAKES

1 lb. hamburger	1/2 c. grated cheese
1/4 c. chopped onion	seasonings to taste
2 eggs, beaten	6 slices whole wheat bread
1/2 c. whole wheat bread crumbs	

Butter slices of bread and place buttered side down in a muffin tin. Shape in. Combine rest of ingredients. Fill muffin tin heaping full with meat mixture so it has the shape of a cupcake. Bake at 350° for 40 min. These cupcakes are good hot or cold.

BARBECUED CHICKEN

Heat a 10 in. iron skillet with 2 T. butter. Dice an onion and fry in butter until slightly brown. Spread 1 qt. canned chicken on top of onions – broth, bones, and all.

Add:

2 T. vinegar	1/4 t. cayenne pepper
1 c. catsup	2 T. sorghum
2 T. Worcestershire sauce	1 T. mustard

Cover and simmer until moisture is almost all absorbed. Serve on buttered bread.

CHICKEN BREASTS

6 chicken breasts, halved	1 c. bread crumbs
1/2 c. butter, melted	1/2 c. grated cheese

Dip chicken in butter, then roll in mix of bread and cheese. Salt if desired. Bake at 350° for 1 hr. or until done. Serves 8.

MOCK COUNTRY SAUSAGE

Cooked brown rice, toasted bread crumbs, celery, chopped walnuts, peanut butter, braised, sliced onions. Flavor with garlic, sage, and salt.

Mold into round balls. Bread and dip in hot oil until brown.

OVEN-FRIED MUSTARD CHICKEN

8 pieces chicken (thigs, legs, or breasts)
1/2 c. butter
2 t. soy sauce
1 T. mustard
2 c. bread crumbs with your favorite seasonings mixed in –
sugg.: salt, pepper, sage, curry, garlic, or onion salt

Melt butter. Add mustard and soy sauce. Dip chicken pieces into butter mixture, then roll in bread crumbs. Bake uncovered at 350° for 1 hour.

CHICKEN TURNOVERS

2 c. wheat flour   1 t. vega-sal
1/2 c. butter   1/2 c. yogurt
1 1/2 c. cooked chicken, turkey, or liver, minced
1 T. butter   1 hard-boiled egg
1/2 c. yogurt
dash of each of vege-sal, black pepper, Spike, paprika, and thyme

To make pastry, mix flour and salt. Blend in butter. Work in 1/2 c. yogurt. Wrap in waxed paper and chill.

To make filling, sauté meat in 1 T. butter for 2 – 3 min. Add egg and seasonings. Remove from heat and add 1/2 c. yogurt. Mix well.

Roll out pastry to 1/4 in. thickness. Cut out turnovers and put 1 T. filling on one side of each round. Wet edges and fold over. Pinch edges to seal. Put on greased cookie sheet and bake at 375° for about 15 min. Serve hot as an appetizer, with soup, or as a snack. Makes 14 to 16.

MAIN DISHES

CRUNCHY CHICKEN

4 c. cooked chicken, cut into bite-size pieces
1/2 c. melted butter   dash of pepper
3/4 c. bread crumbs   1/2 t. Spike
1/2 c. grated Colby cheese   1 t. Vege-sal

 Mix all ingredients together. Place on a cookie sheet that is covered with lightly greased tin foil. Bake in 400° oven for 10 min. Serve.

YUMMY HAMBURGERS

1/2 c. chopped onion   1 t. prepared mustard
1 1/2 lb. hamburger   2 T. oil
2 T. wheat flour   6 T. catsup
1 c. sour cream   1/4 t. pepper

 Brown onion in oil, add meat and brown. Add rest of ingredients. Simmer 5 min. Serve on buns. Serves 8.

VEGETABLE PIZZA

1. Prepare pizza crust recipe on page 61. Spread on a greased 14" pizza pan.
2. Spread a layer of baked beans on crust (Boston Baked Beans, page 56), or refried beans can be used if warmed first to make them spreadable.
3. Spread with 1 pint pizza sauce.
4. Bake in a 350° oven for 20 minutes. Take out and sprinkle generously with cheese. Put back in and bake 10 more minutes.
5. Cut pizza slices and serve with grated cabbage.
6. Top with your favorite salad dressing. Our first choice is sweet 'n sour. This pizza is truly delicious!

For variation you can add sour cream on top of the beans before putting on pizza sauce. You can also substitute regular tossed salad for the cabbage. Or sprinkle crushed corn chips or croutons on top for a special touch.

PIZZA DOUGH

1/2 c. warm water to dissolve	1 T. yeast
Add:	
6 T. butter or 1/3 c. oil	1 t. vega-sal or 1 t. garlic salt
1 c. wheat flour	1/2 c. cornmeal

Dough should be soft but not stiff. Spread out with fingers in a 12 in. greased pie plate or 2 smaller ones. You will need to dip your fingers in flour every so often so the dough doesn't stick to your fingers. Bake in 425° oven for 20 - 25 min. Fill with filling of your choice. We like a hamburger mixture with pizza sauce, etc. Then put Colby cheese on top to melt. Very good.

RICE PIZZA

2 c. cooked rice	1/2 c. onion
2 T. melted butter	1/2 t. salt
1 egg, beaten	1/4 t. oregano
hamburger	cheese
1 c. pizza sauce	

Combine rice, butter, and eggs. Line the bottom of a 12" pizza pan with the rice mixture, pressing it with the back of a tablespoon. Make a run around the edge about 1/4" high. Bake at 350° for 10 minutes. Arrange meat in rice crust. Mix sauce and onion and spoon over meat. Top with cheese, and put back in oven until melted.

PIZZA CRUST▾

2 c. wheat flour (may use part cornmeal)	
2 t. baking powder	1 t. salt or 2 t. garlic salt
1/4 c. oil	2/3 c. water

Mix and press onto greased pizza pan. If you want a softer crust, add 1 egg. Add a little more flour to compensate for the extra moisture.

MAIN DISHES

No more tears when peeling onions if you place them in the deep freeze for 4 or 5 minutes.

MAIN DISHES

Potatoes will bake in a hurry if they are boiled in salted water for 10 minutes before popping into a very hot oven.

POTATO KUGEL

3 - 4 peeling size potatoes, peeled

2 medium carrots, peeled	1 slice whole wheat bread
3/4 c. powdered milk	2 t. salt
1 onion	1/8 t. sage
2 eggs, beaten	3 T. oil

Grate vegetables and drain off liquid. Stir in remaining ingredients, adding powdered milk gradually to avoid any lumps. Spread into greased glass cake pan. Bake at 350° for 50 - 55 min. When kugel is nearly done it will be brown around the edges and test done like a cake. Arrange slices of Colby cheese over top of kugel and return to oven to melt cheese. Remove from oven and cut into 2 - 3 in. squares. Top each square with yogurt or sour cream if desired.

BAKED CHICKEN PIE

2 c. chicken	3/4 c. cream
2 c. potatoes	5 c. chicken broth
diced and cooked	1/2 c. celery
3 T. butter	salt and seasoning
4 T. flour	
Batter:	
2 c. flour	1/2 t. salt
2 heaping t. baking powder	1 egg
1 c. milk	

Melt butter, add flour and blend until smooth. Then add broth, cream, and salt to taste. Bring to a boil. Add chicken, celery, and potatoes. Bring to a boil. Mix batter and drop into broth. Bake for 20 - 30 min.

CHINESE GLOB

1 lb. hamburger
1 c. chopped celery
1 c. brown rice
1 c. chopped onion
1 qt. gravy

   Cook rice and fry hamburger and onions together. Then mix all ingredients and season to taste. Bake for 1 hour.

RICE MEATBALL STEW

3 c. water
1 t. basil
1/8 t. garlic salt
   Simmer 40 min.
1 lb. green beans (frozen)
1 qt. tomato chunks
1 1/4 c. brown rice
1/2 t. salt

1/2 recipe Italian Meatballs
1/2 c. spaghetti sauce

   Stir into rice. Heat enough so that beans thaw.
   Serve with sprouts, carrot sticks, and cornmeal biscuits.

TIME SAVER SUNDAY DINNER

1 qt. canned green beans
1 qt. canned meatballs
1 pt. canned carrots
1 pt. tomato juice
1 1/2 - 2 t. salt
1 c. brown rice
1 onion, diced

1 - 3 c. water, depending on how much liquid is with vegetables and meat

   Put all together in a large covered casserole and simmer in a slow oven for 3 - 4 hours. This is delicious with homemade creamed cottage cheese.

   Note: If you don't want this in the oven while in church, get the rice ready beforehand and then it can all be quickly heated up when ready to eat.

MAIN DISHES

If you've oversalted a kettle of stew or soup, drop in a raw potato (cut up), It will absorb the salt

RICE-VEGETABLE CASSEROLE▾

2/3 c. raw brown rice
1/4 - 1/2 c. green or yellow split peas or lentils
2 c. deboned, canned chicken and broth
3 c. water (can use part soy milk)
1 small onion
1 bit of parsley or some Parsley Patch seasoning
1 t. soy sauce
1/2 t. vega-sal

Combine all ingredients in a casserole dish and bake at 350° for 1 1/2 hours.

Note: If the chicken is omitted, add 1/2 c. or more water. Also carrots, celery, or peas may be used instead of lentils or split peas.

BAKED CRACKER CRUMB POTATOES▾

Scrub potatoes and cut in halves and fourths. Dip potato pieces in melted butter and roll in cracker crumbs to which seasonings have been added. Arrange on cookie sheet and bake at 350° for 1 1/2 hours.

BAKED POTATO STICKS▾

3 medium peeling potatoes
1/4 c. butter
Salt to taste

Peel potatoes and cut lengthwise 1/2" strips. Roll in melted butter and place on cookie sheet. Sprinkle with salt. Cover with tin foil and bake at 350° for 1 hr. Take off foil for the last 5 - 10 min. to let the sticks get a little crisp.

ITALIAN MEATBALLS (No Meat)

1 1/2 c. wheat flour	1 T. basil
2 c. bread crumbs	1 t. thyme
2 T. parsley flakes	1/8 t. garlic salt
Stir altogether.	
1/4 c. roasted sunflower seeds	2 T. lemon juice
3 T. nutritional yeast flakes	1 c. water
1/3 c. oatmeal	2 T. ketchup
1/8 t. garlic powder	1 t. salt

Blend well and pour into first mixture. Add 1/2 c. peanut butter. Stir together well and form into balls 1" round. Bake at 350° for 35 min. Also freezes well.

MEATBALL PIZZA

1 1/2 lbs. bread dough
   Roll out and place on a large greased cookie sheet.
1 qt. thick tomato sauce
   Spread on dough.
1 grated onion   oregano to taste
   Sprinkle all over sauce
1/2 recipe Italian Meatballs
   Crumble over top. Bake at 425° for 15 - 20 min.

HOT CHICKEN SANDWICHES

2 c. chopped, cooked chicken	1/4 c. finely chopped onion
3 chopped hard boiled eggs	1/2 c. homemade Miracle Whip
2 c. chicken gravy	

Bake at 350° for 25 minutes and spread on warmed whole wheat bread.

MAIN DISHES

Try arrowroot as a thickener. 1 level T. thickens 1 c. liquid to a medium stage.

BURRITOS

Another dish that can be made with tortillas (see tortilla recipe). Take fried tortillas and spread with mashed beans (open a jar of October beans or use leftover baked beans or whatever is handy). Sprinkle with grated cheese or omit cheese. Roll up and place on a cookie sheet. Warm burritos in oven for 10 min.

Variation: CHEESE CRISPS can be made by using only the cheese (not the beans). Roll up the tortillas and warm in oven until cheese melts. At the table, each person can put a small amount of bean, a little chili sauce, and a little sour cream on their place. These may be used to accompany the Cheese Crisp.

TACOS▾

1 c. flour   1/2 c. cornmeal
1/4 t. salt   1 egg
1 1/2 c. cold water

Mix together. Fry on both sides (paper thin) in greaseless skillet. Can put in low over to crisp.

Filling:

Brown 1 1/2 lbs. turkey burger. Stir in 2 T. chili powder, salt to taste.

Sauce:

2 c. tomato juice   1 onion, chopped
1 pepper, chopped   1/2 t. salt
1/2 t. red pepper   1 t. garlic

Cook until thickened. Spread burger on tacos, then sauce. Top with shredded lettuce.

TACOS OR TORTILLAS

3/4 c. cornmeal	1 t. salt
1 c. wheat flour	3 T. oil
1 1/2 c. water	2 eggs

Fry like pancakes, only bigger. Tip the frying pan around so the batter spreads into a thin, round tortilla, or spread thin with back of spoon.

Top with: mashed beans, browned hamburger, chopped lettuce, tomatoes and onions, grated cheese, catsup, and hot sauce. We let each person fix their own taco at the table.

HOMEMADE TACOS▼

1 c. flour (1/2 oat and 1/2 whole wheat)

1/2 c.cornmeal	1 egg
1/4 t. salt	1 1/2 c. cold water

Mix and fry paper thin in greaseless griddle until done but not hard. Drape over oven rack in warm oven until crisp.

Brown ground turkey and season as you like. Layer meat, tomato sauce, lettuce, tomatoes, etc. on tacos.

CORN FRITTERS▼

1 qt. creamed corn	1 egg
1/2 c. cornmeal	2 c. whole wheat flour
2 t. baking powder	1 t. salt

Mix and fry on hot skillet. More flour may be added if it is not the right consistency.

This is good served with tomato gravy.

MAIN DISHES

When cooking peas, use only half the salt and add crushed marjoram leaves.

MAIN DISHES

To determine whether an egg is hard boiled, spin it. If it spins, it is hard boiled; if it wobbles and will not spin it is raw.

SAVORY EGG PUFF

1/2 c. chopped onion	5 eggs
1 1/2 c. cottage cheese	1/4 t. sage
3/4 c. cubed cheese	1 t. salt
1/4 c. wheat flour	3 T. milk
1 t. baking powder	2 T. yogurt
1/4 t. curry powder	

Put all ingredients in blender and blend for 1 min. Pour into baking dish and bake at 350° for 45 min.

OATMEAL DRESSING▾

3 c. regular oats	1 onion, cut up fine
2 c. diced celery	3 T. butter
1 - 2 c. beef or chicken broth	seasoning to taste

Sauté onion and celery in butter. Add oatmeal and cook, stirring constantly until oatmeal browns slightly. Add sage. Mix well. Add broth, just a little at a time so it will not stick together. Continue to cook until oatmeal is cooked and dressing is just moist enought o still toss lightly in skillet.

This dressing is very good, but tricky to make. If you add the liquid too quickly, you end up with one big mushy mess. Add no more than 2 T. at a time.

BREAD TOPPING

3/4 c. chopped onion	1 c. chopped celery
3/4 c. butter	2 t. salt
1/4 t. red pepper	1/2 t. curry powder
9 c. bread crumbs	2 t. Indo

Sauté onions and celery in butter until soft. Sprinkle seasonings over bread and toss lightly. Add butter, onions and celery and toss again.

This mixture can be used to top casseroles or with chicken and fish.

DANDELION GRAVY

Pour some safflower oil in a frying pan. Add enough flour to make a smooth paste. Brown nicely. Add some cold water, stirring quickly until smooth. Add milk gradually and cook to thicken. Take off of burner and add salt to taste and some vinegar and honey. Finally, add a few diced hard boiled eggs and chopped fresh young dandelion greens to suit your taste.

This is good gravy for potatoes cooked in their skins.

DELICIOUS BROWN GRAVY

1/2 c. butter	2/3 c. flour (scant)
4 T. nutritional yeast	1 tsp. salt
4 c. water	freshly ground black pepper to taste

Melt butter, let it brown. Stir in flour a little at a time. Cook briefly. Mixture should be bubbly. Add water, all at once and begin stirring with wire whisk. Add the yeast flakes, salt and pepper as you stir. Cook over medium heat until gravy thickens. Very good on mashed potatoes, home fries, baked potatoes, rice or in casseroles. Vege-sal can also be added. Makes 1 qt.

MAIN DISHES

Frying fish? Roll in cornmeal and sprinkle with Indo. Tastes like breaded fish.

MAIN DISHES

Whenever any recipe asks for salt, use sea salt. Be careful what kind of sea salt is used for it may be no healthier than any other kind of salt. If it is free flowing and does not cake or get lumpy, you may be sure it has been overheated, thus killing the trace minerals that had been there. Also watch the label for chemicals and additives.

WHITE SAUCE

3 T. whole wheat flour	1 c. water
3 T. butter	1 1/2 c. cream or milk
salt	

Melt butter in pan. Add flour. Cook over low heat 3 - 4 minutes. Cooking eliminates the flour and water pasty taste. Add cream and water.

This may be used as a base for cream soups. Add 1 c. mushrooms for mushroom soup and 1 c. celery for celery soup.

Make large batches and can it. Very handy for casseroles.

TOMATO GRAVY

Bring tomato juice to a boil and thicken with flour and cream or milk. Add a pinch of baking soda first to keep from curdling. Season with salt and other seasonings if you prefer.

TOMATO GRAVY

Sauté chopped onions in butter until slightly clear. Add flour and brown like you would for "pan gravy." Then add tomato juice and milk or cream. Season to taste.

Tomato gravy is good with pancakes, cornbread, fried corn mush, scrambled eggs or omelet, and potato cakes.

SOUR CREAM FOR BAKED POTATOES

Soften 8 oz. cream cheese.
Add 1/3 c. light cream; beat until fluffy.
 Add:

1 1/2 t. lemon juice	1/2 t. garlic salt

 Blend well.

BARBECUE SAUCE

2 c. lemon juice	2 t. poultry seasoning
1 t. garlic salt	salt and pepper to taste

 Mix altogether. This may be used for outdoor grilling, or pour over chicken in roaster and bake.

BEAN SOUP

1/2 c. diced celery	1 little onion
1 c. browned hamburger	salt and pepper to taste
2 T. catsup	1 pt. water
1/2 c. diced carrot	

 Cook until done, adding a pint of milk to a quart of soup to serve.

EASIEST SPLIT PEA SOUP

2 c. split peas

 Put in a soup pot, after rinsing and cover 1" with water. Bring to boil, then simmer on medium heat for 1 hour, stirring frequently. Peas will break down and soup will become thick and creamy. Add water to desired consistency and flavor with garlic and onion salt, Vege sal or other salt.

A left over baked potato can be rebaked if you dip it in water and bake in a 350° oven for about 20 minutes.

In late fall when you have plenty of sweet green or red peppers and onions available, take them and chop them up in a salsa master. Measure and package in labeled ziplock bags and pop them in the freezer. These are convenient when making winter soups. Onions must be stored in a Rubbermaid container if you don't want your whole freezer to smell like them.

MAIN DISHES

S erve soup with cornbread or muffins instead of crackers.

KALE - LENTIL SOUP

1 bunch of kale, coarsely chopped

1 onion, minced · 4 c. water

3 garlic cloves, minced · part of fresh jalapeño pepper

1 can tomatoes in juice · 1/2 t. cumin powder (optional)

1 leafy stalk of celery, chopped

1 c. lentils · vega-sal to taste

Rinse lentils and place everything in a large kettle. Bring to a boil. Cover and simmer for 1 hour.

BROCCOLI SOUP

1 c. fresh or frozen broccoli, cut up

1/4 c. celery, cut fine

1 T. chopped onion

1 qt. water

Put all together in a saucepan and bring to a boil. Simmer until tender. Add more water if necessary. Make a paste of 1 T. flour and a little milk. Add to vegetables and bring to a boil. Remove from heat. Add several slices of cheese and let set until melted. If desired, potatoes may be added. Leftover mashed potatoes may be added just before cheese.

HOMEMADE MUSHROOM SOUP

Brown over high heat 2 - 3 minutes:

1 pkg. mushrooms · 1/2 stick butter

Add:

2 T. flour · salt

1 qt. milk

Cook until thickened.

MUSHROOM SOUP

1 can mushrooms (chopped)
1/3 c. each celery and carrots, chopped fine
a little onion and garlic   salt and pepper to taste
1 pt. beef broth   3 T. catsup
2 soup cans water   1/2 c. milk
1 soup can milk   2 T. wheat flour

   Combine all ingredients except the 2 last ones. Cook until tender, then add milk and flour to thicken.

CHILI SOUP

1 large onion   1 T. chili powder
2 c. hamburger   2 c. uncooked whole wheat noodles
1 qt. tomato juice   2 T. butter
2 c. red kidney beans   2 T. sorghum

   Precook noodles. Fry onion and hamburger in butter until brown. Add remaining ingredients, except noodles. Bring to a boil and simmer 10 min. Add salt to taste, then add cooked noodles. Stir and serve.

CREAM OF CELERY SOUP

   Melt 1 T. butter and add 2 T. cornstarch and 1/2 t. salt.
   Blend and slowly add 1/4 c. milk. Bring to a boil. Add 1/2 to 1 stick celery, finely chopped. Cook until celery is soft, stirring frequently.
   Can be used in recipes asking for cream of celery or cream of mushroom soup. Can also be made in large amounts and canned.

MAIN DISHES

MAIN DISHES

Use brown rice flour to make noodles instead of white flour.

LENTIL RICE SOUP

1/2 c. lentils   1/4 t. dill weed
1 c . brown rice   1 t. salt
1/2 onion, thinly sliced   broth or water
1 small clove garlic, crushed

   Wash lentils. Bring rice, lentils, and liquid to a boil. Add onions, garlic, salt, and dill. Reduce heat and simmer until rice is tender – about 1 hour. Add diced celery and carrots and cook just until tender.

MILLET SOUP

1 qt. meat stock   1 c. millet
1 sm. head cabbage   1/2 t. salt
3/4 c. chopped celery   1 T. butter
2 c. shredded carrots   parsley

   Cook millet for 15 minutes. Add vegetables. Simmer on low heat for 30 minutes or until done.
   Leftover vegetables may be used instead of cabbage.

CREAMY POTATO SOUP

3 c. diced potatoes
1/4 c. onions, finely chopped
1 c. celery, finely chopped

   Cook until tender and mash well (do not drain water). Add 2 T. browned butter, and enough milk to make the amount of soup you need.
   Mix 1/2 c. milk with 1 T. cornstarch until smooth. Add to slowly boiling soup, stirring constantly until thickened. Add parsley and other seasonings to taste.

TOMATO SOUP

1 1/2 gal. tomatoes (cut up)

Cover with water. Add 2 large onions, 1/4 c. salt (scant), and 1/4 c. maple syrup. Cook for 20 minutes and put through stainer.

Add:

1/2 piece butter	1 large bunch celery
1/4 t. cloves	1/4 t. nutmeg

3/4 c. flour mixed with a little water

Cook until slightly thickened and cold pack 1 hour.

TOMATO SOUP▾

4 T. olive oil	1/2 c. parsley, chopped
4 carrots, peeled and diced	6 leaves of fresh basil
4 stalks celery, finely diced	salt or vega-sal and pepper to taste
3 medium onions, chopped	

14 large, ripe tomatoes or 3 qts. canned tomatoes with juice

Heat the oil in a large kettle. Sauté the carrots, celery, and onions for about 20 min. or until tender. Add tomatoes and continue cooking for 25 - 30 min. or longer. Stir in parsley and basil. Season with salt and pepper and cook a minute longer. Serve or freeze.

CREAM OF CHICKEN SOUP

1/2 c. butter	9 c. boiling water
6 heaping T. flour	1 pt. chicken broth
1 t. salt	1 c. rich milk
4 t. Nutri-Soup	parsley flakes

Melt butter in kettle and blend in flour. Gradually add 9 c. boiling water and stir until smooth. If you want it thicker, add more flour, as you would to gravy. Now add the rest of the ingredients.

*Nutri-Soup can be bought at the health food store, taking the place of chicken soup base. Other seasonings may be used instead also.

Add a pinch of baking soda to tomato soup or anything with tomatoes in which you want to add milk or cream. It will keep it from curdling.

MAIN DISHES

A little salt sprinkled into the frying pan will prevent spattering.

MEATLESS POTATO SOUP

9 medium potatoes	salt
2 large onions	onion salt
1 1/2 c. peas, frozen	pepper
2 T. butter	

Peel 4 potatoes and slice into small kettle, cover with water, bring to boil and simmer till soft. Peel the remaining 5 potatoes and cube. Mince the onions and put these in a kettle with the potatoes. Barely cover with water, bring to boil, and simmer with till tender (not mushy). Drain the potato water in the small kettle into a jar. Mash these potatoes and dump them into the large kettle. Stir these in till the soup thickens. Add the peas and butter. Add salt, onion salt, pepper till it tastes right. Delicious!

DELICIOUS TOFU SOUP

2 medium onions, chopped	3 T. butter
1 pt. green beans, sliced small	3/4 qt. tomato juice
2 c. kidney beans w/liquid if using canned beans	Italian seasoning dried parsley
1 c. tofu	pizza sauce

Squeeze tofu to remove excess water, then crumble. Sauté onions in butter. Add beans, tofu and tomato juice. Add seasonings. Yummy!

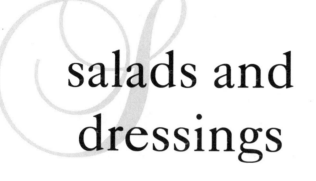

salads and dressings

SALADS AND DRESSINGS

Add shredded carrots to tuna, chicken, or turkey salad sandwiches. They also give extra taste and nutrients to corned beef, ham and cheese, and peanut butter sandwiches.

STUFFED TOMATOES

Mix:

2 c. Miracle Whip	1/4 c. finely chopped celery
1/4 c. chopped cucumber	1 c. finely chopped chicken
1 T. finely chopped onion	or turkey

Cut 6 tomatoes into 6 wedges, each just halfway down and spread open slightly. Fill with mixture. Serve on lettuce leaf and garnish with sliced cucumber and green pepper rings.

MIXED BEAN SALAD

1/2 c. kidney beans	1/2 c. navy beans
1/2 c. garbanzo beans	3/4 c. brown rice

Soak each one overnight and cook separately. Drain and mix. Chill.

Dressing:

1 c. olive oil	1 onion, chopped fine
1/3 c. vinegar	sea salt and mustard

EASY CABBAGE SLAW

2 blender pitchers of very coarse cabbage pieces

Fill 1/2 - 3/4 full of water. Whirl in blender until finely chopped. Drain into colander or strainer. Squeeze out excess water with hands and put into a bowl. Add chopped tomatoes. Grated carrots may be added to stretch it, too. Add raisins and pour your favorite dressing over it and mix. Serves 4 - 6.

STUFFED PEPPERS▾

Slice peppers in half. Clean and wash.

4 Ryvata crackers, broken

    (these may be purchased at the health food store)

2 hardboiled eggs, mashed   1 bunch parsley, chopped

1 chopped tomato   1 T. blender mayonnaise

    Mix and season with vega-sal. Stuff peppers and serve.

APPLE-CABBAGE SLAW

1/2 c. sour cream or plain yogurt

2 t. honey   2 c. sliced apples

1/2 t. salt   3 c. shredded cabbage

1/2 t. prepared mustard   1/2 t. pepper (optional)

1 1/2 t. lemon juice (optional)   1 T. vinegar

    Mix sour cream or yogurt and seasonings. Sprinkle lemon juice over apples to prevent darkening. Mix apples and cabbage together. Pour dressing over mixture and toss lightly.

HEALTHY HAYSTACK▾

    On each plate or in separate bowls, put:

lettuce and sprouts

1 shredded carrot

1 stalk chopped celery

1 small tomato

shredded natural cheese or cottage cheese (could substitute yogurt)

1 sliced hardboiled egg (optional)

small handful sunflower seeds or sliced almonds

    Variation: Top with brown rice and chicken.

SALADS AND DRESSINGS

Onions – slice thin and sprinkle with Indo or honey and let stand a half day. They will not be so strong and they will make good sandwiches. Get vidalia onions if you can – they are not so strong.

SALADS AND DRESSINGS

Onions can be minced fine, wrapped in cloth, and wrung out under cold running water until the sharp taste is gone.

SOYBEAN - CHEESE SALAD

2 c. cooked soybeans, drained   1 c. cooked, diced carrots
1/2 c. grated cheese   (can be grated raw, too)
1 c. finely chopped celery   1/2 c. diced cucumbers
   Mix with dressing and place in salad dish. Top with slices of tomatoes and sprigs of parsley.

VINEGAR ONIONS

   Mix vinegar and water about half and half. Add salt to taste. Thinly slice onions and cover with brine a few hours. Just before serving, drain brine and eat the onion with bread and butter. This makes the onions milder.

RICE SALAD

1 1/2 c. cooked brown rice
   Cool and add:
4 tomatoes, diced   1/2 c. celery, chopped
1/2 green pepper, diced
   Dressing:
juice of 1 lemon   1/2 t. paprika
2 1/2 T. chopped parsley   pinch of salt
5 T. olive oil   1 T. catsup
2/3 c. plain yogurt
   Combine all ingredients and blend well. Pour over rice and vegetables.

RICE SALAD

3 c. cooked brown rice
   Cool and add:
1 c. cooked chicken bits   1/2 c. finely chopped celery
1 1/2 c. sliced strawberries
   Dressing:
3/4 c. homemade miracle whip (pg. 86)
1/2 t. sea salt   1 t. mustard
1 t. lemon juice   1/3 c. yogurt
   Combine all ingredients and blend well. Pour over rice and vegetables.

MAKE-AHEAD SALAD

In a large glass bowl, layer the following:

1 torn-up head lettuce   1 medium finely chopped onion
1 pkg. frozen peas (not cooked)
1 small head cauliflower   6 hard-boiled eggs, sliced

Seal with mayonnaise over entire top (this is the secret to a crisp salad later – to completely seal the top).

Sprinkle grated cheese over the top. Cover with Saran Wrap and refrigerate overnight.

This is a wonderful last minute time-saver when you have guests.

SALAD EGGS

Hard boiled eggs taste better if not boiled too hard nor too long – no longer than 10 minutes. If you have plenty of time, just bring your water to the boiling point and then turn the burner off and let set half an hour.

For easy peeling, be sure to use older eggs. If you have only fresh eggs, don't put the eggs into the water until it is boiling and add salt to your water.

When the eggs are cooled and peeled, cut in half and remove yolk. Mash the yolk and mix with mayonnaise. For a variety, try adding any of these: wheat germ, bran, nuts, sesame seeds, mushrooms, chopped green peppers, finely chopped onions, sprouts, and celery.

STUFFED EGGS▾

Cook and peel eggs. Season to taste with:
dry mustard
celery seed
vege-sal or salt and pepper
enough blender mayonnaise for creamy texture.

Fresh egg shells are rough and chalky; old eggs are smooth and shiny.

SALADS AND DRESSINGS

To remove the core from a head of lettuce, hit the core end once against the counter sharply. The core will loosen and pull out easily.

HEALTHY POTATO SALAD

6 potatoes, cooked and diced	1/3 c. plain yogurt
1 onion, chopped fine	1/2 c. milk
2 hard-boiled eggs, diced	1/4 c. parsley
1 c. cottage cheese	dash of red pepper

Mix yogurt and milk. Place 1/3 of potatoes in a bowl and cover with each of the ingredients. Repeat. Cover and refrigerate 12 - 24 hours. When ready to serve, toss well and top with a sprinkling of parsley.

POTATO SUPPER SALAD

5 c. diced, cooked potatoes	1/2 c. thinly sliced radishes
1/2 c. finely chopped celery	1/4 c. chopped green pepper
1/4 c. finely chopped onions	

Sprinkle with salt or herbal seasoning. Lightly mix in 1/4 c. French dressing and chill 2 or 3 hours. Just before serving, fold in 1 1/2 c. yogurt. Place lettuce on serving platter with potato mixture on top. Garnish with 3 hard cooked, sliced eggs. Serves 8.

POTATO SALAD▾

To potatoes, add to taste –

blender mayonnaise	celery salt
celery seed	dry mustard
salt	lemon juice
chopped eggs, celery, and onions	

CARROT SALAD

2 envelopes gelatin dissolved in 1/2 c. cold water
  When dissolved, add:

1/4 c. hot water	2 c. apple juice

  Set aside until it is about the consistency of egg whites. Stir in:

2 c. finely grated carrots	1 pt. crushed pineapple
1/4 c. finely chopped celery	with its juice
3/4 c. sunflower seeds	1/2 c. honey

QUICK ORANGE JELLO

3 T. unflavored gelatin	12 oz. can frozen orange juice
1/2 c. cold water	(no sugar added)
2 c. boiling water	4 c. fruit – peaches, bananas,
2 c. cold water or fruit juice	pineapple, etc.

  In 3 qt. mixing bowl, soften gelatin in cold water. Then pour boiling water over gelatin, stirring until completely dissolved. Add cold water or fruit juice and frozen orange juice. As juice melts, gelatin will become thick. Add fruit. Can be served in 20 min., or wait until set to desired firmness.

  Note: This makes a large bowl full, depending ont the amount of fruit you add.

ORANGE SALAD

2 heaping T. gelatin	1 pt. crushed pineapple
1 c. boiling orange juice	1 c. chopped pecans
1 pt. homemade ice cream	1 sliced banana

  Dissolve gelatin in hot juice. Add other ingredients and chill to thicken.

SALADS AND DRESSINGS

Add sprouts to chicken, tuna, egg or turkey sandwiches.

SALADS AND DRESSINGS

L entil sprouts go well with eggs, soups, meat loafs, and salads.

FRUIT SALAD GELATIN

1 3/4 T. plain gelatin dissolved in 2 c. orange juice*

2 c. orange juice heated to boiling and poured over dissolved gelatin

Stir thoroughly. Add 2 c. more orange juice. Chill until partly thickened. Add fruit, such as bananas, grapes, orange sections, or pineapple. Or make a carrot-jello salad by adding grated carrots and crushed pineapple.

Variation: Use pineapple juice instead of orange juice.

Frozen orange juice concentrate, made up according to directions, or with a little less water, works well.

HEALTH SALAD

1 envelope unflavored gelatin dissolved in 1/4 c. cold water

Boil 1 c. apple juice and pour over dissolved gelatin. Cool and add:

1 cup apples, cut up (do not peel)   1/2 c. celery, diced

1 c. applesauce   1/2 c. nuts

APPLE PEAR SALAD

2 apples, sliced	lettuce leaves
1 stalk celery, cut fine	2 pears, sliced
2 T. lemon juice	1 T. honey
1/4 t. salt	1/4 t. pumpkin pie spice

Mix apples, pears, and celery. Shake lemon juice, honey, salt, and spice in tightly covered container. Pour over apple mixture; toss until evenly coated. Cover and refrigerate at least 1 hour. Arrange salad on lettuce leaves to serve. Serves 8.

APPLE SALAD

1 c. honey	2 c. water
2 T. flour	2 eggs, beaten
1/3 t. salt	

Cook until thickened and add 2 scant t. vanilla. Add 2 T. butter. Cool and pour over a salad of:

apples	nuts
pineapple	raisins
cheese	

APPLE SALAD

8 apples, peeled and diced
1 c. unsweetened, shredded coconut
1 c. raisins

Put the three above ingredients in a bowl and mix with dressing.
Dressing:

1 c. peanut butter (natural)	honey to taste
3/4 c. milk	maple flavoring (optional)

RAINBOW FRUIT SALAD

Any fruit in season, or use drained canned fruit (the more variation, the better).

watermelon	raspberries	cherries
blueberries	peaches	pears
blackberries	cantaloupe	apples

Cut each fruit into bite size pieces. Pour 1 - 2 cups yogurt on top, depending on your family size. Toss lightly and serve.

Note: bananas and raisins could be added, also.

When soaking seeds for sprouting, save the first water you pour off. Use for a drink or in gravies, to cook vegetables or stews. It has a lot of nutritional value.

SPECIAL SALAD

3 oz. unflavored gelatin	2 T. honey
1 3/4 c. boiling water	1 c. crushed pineapple, drained
2 T. vinegar	1 c. grated cheese
1 T. lemon juice	1 c. heavy cream, whipped

Dissolve gelatin in boiling water. Add vinegar, lemon juice, and honey. Chill until slightly thickened. Fold in pineapple, cheese, and whipped cream. Pour into mold and chill.

SANDWICH SPREAD

4 hard-boiled eggs, chopped	1 clove garlic
1/2 c. yogurt	1 T. parsley
1 small onion, finely chopped	1/2 tomato, chunked

Use for sandwiches or spread on crackers.

HOMEMADE MIRACLE WHIP

3/4 c. canola oil	1 T. lemon juice
1/3 c. honey	1/2 t. mustard
1 egg plus water to make 3/4 cup	
2 t. salt	

Beat water and egg *thoroughly* with egg beater. Cook the following in a qt. saucepan:

2/3 c. whole wheat flour
1 cup water
1/3 c. vinegar

Bring to a boil, then blend in the other ingredients. Beat hard until smooth. Makes 1 qt.

Note: This recipe may be used in any other recipe that calls for Miracle Whip.

MAYONNAISE

1 egg, beaten
1/2 t. sea salt
1/4 t. red pepper
2 T. honey

4 t. vinegar
7 t. lemon juice
1 1/2 c. oil

Beat all ingredients together except the oil. Then, *very slowly,* add the oil and *beat.* It will become thicker with more oil, but it *must* be added slowly. We omit the lemon juice and pepper. More eggs may be used if desired.

BLENDER MAYONNAISE▾

2 eggs
1 t. salt

1 1/4 t. dry mustard
1/2 t. paprika

Beat until thoroughly mixed and add 1 T. lemon juice. Continute to beat 2 c. oil and 1 T. lemon juice.

Slowly pour in half of the oil, while beating at high speed. If you add the oil too fast, the mayonnaise will curdle. Slowly add lemon juice and remainder of the oil and beat until smooth and creamy.

Note: This is also good as a dip for vegetables.

BLENDER MAYONNAISE▾

2 eggs at room temperature
2 T. fresh squeezed lemon juice (ReaLemon can be used)
1/4 t. sea salt
1 1/4 c. unrefined vegetable oil

Combine all ingredients *except oil* in blender at high speed for 1 minute. Slowly add oil. Store in glass jar in refrigerator. This actually gets thick like the consistency of Miracle Whip.

More juice can be taken from a lemon if it is first warmed slightly in oven.

SALADS AND DRESSINGS

When celery or lettuce loses its crispness, place it in a pan of cold water with a raw potato in it. After a while it will be crisp again.

COOKED DRESSING

2 T. honey   1 T. flour
1/2 t. salt   1/4 t. mustard
2 beaten eggs   1/2 c. yogurt
3 T. vinegar
   Cook together until thickened. Good on cabbage or cooked vegetables.

COTTAGE CHEESE DRESSING▾

1 c. cottage cheese   3 hard-boiled eggs, minced
1 c. yogurt   4 T. minced green pepper
4 T. lemon juice   Indo (seasoning)
   Beat cottage cheese with egg beater, add rest of ingredients and blend well.

CUCUMBER DRESSING▾

   Beat until fluffy:
2 egg yolks   1/4 t. mustard
1/4 t. salt   1/4 t. paprika
   Slowly beat in:
1 c. yogurt   1 T. lemon juice
   This is enough for 2 unpeeled, sliced cucumbers. Put fresh parsley on top.

FRENCH DRESSING

1 t. lemon juice
1/4 t. honey
1/4 t. paprika

4 T. olive oil
1/4 t. salt

Mix 1 1/2 T. oil with the dry ingredients. Stir well and add the lemon juice. As the dressing thickens through stirring, add the rest of the oil and a little garlic flavor if you like.

Note: This may be used in any recipe that calls for French dressing.

LETTUCE DRESSING

1 c. cottage cheese
1 t. oregano
1/2 t. thyme
1 T. catsup
1 T. honey
3 T. olive oil

1 t. celery seed
1 t. garlic powder
1/2 t. onion salt
3 T. vinegar
1 t. mustard

Beat until smooth. If too thick, thin with equal parts oil and vinegar.

MEXICAN SALAD DRESSING

1/2 c. maple syrup
1 medium chopped onion
1 c. oil
3 t. mustard

1/3 c. vinegar
1 t. celery seed
1/4 t. pepper
1 T. Miracle Whip (homemade pg.86)

Combine all ingredients and beat together

SALADS AND DRESSINGS

Mung bean sprouts are best when 1 1/2 to 3 inches long.

SALADS AND DRESSINGS

OIL DRESSING (FOR LETTUCE SALAD)

1/3 c. oil	scant 1/4 c. honey
1/4 c. vinegar	1/4 c. water
1/2 t. salt	

Mix altogether and serve over a bowl of cut-up lettuce. Yummy!

TOMATO DRESSING

1 c. yogurt	1 c. grated cheese
2 T. vinegar	1 t. caraway seed

Mix and chill. Serve on sliced tomatoes.

SWEET AND SOUR DRESSING

1/2 c. honey	1 T. homemade Miracle Whip
1/2 c. oil	1 medium onion
2 t. mustard	1/4 c. water
1/4 c. vinegar	1 t. celery seed
1 t. salt	

Combine all ingredients and beat together until smooth.

SWEET AND SOUR DRESSING

1/2 c. honey	2 T. vinegar
1/2 c. oil	2 T. water
1 T. Miracle Whip	1 t. salt
2 t. mustard	1 t. celery seed
1 medium onion, chopped fine	

Combine all ingredients and beat together

SALAD DRESSING

2 - 3 T. fresh, squeezed lemon juice

1/3 - 1/2 c. oil (olive, safflower, sesame, sunflower, or avocado)

Whip the oil and lemon juice together for a creamy dressing.

Note: Whenever you are using oil, use the unrefined, cold-pressed variety, for it is the most easily digested.

If desired, the following seasonings may be added to the basic recipe:

1/4 - 1/2 t. salt

1/4 - 1/2 t. seasoning salt (Spike is one of the best seasoning salts.)

1 t. - 1 T. tamari, a concentrated soy sauce that is quite salty and should be used sparingly

1 clove garlic

1/4 - 1 t. herbs (oregano, basil, thyme, tarrogen, or parsley)

1 - 2 T. mayonnaise

1/2 - 1 t. mustard

THOUSAND ISLAND DRESSING

1 c. yogurt	1 T. minced onion
2 egg yolks, well beaten	1 T. minced green pepper
1/2 t. mustard	1 hard-cooked, chopped egg
dash of paprika	1 T. honey
dash of cayenne	1 T. vinegar
2 T. catsup	salt

Combine all ingredients in bowl and beat together until smooth.

THOUSAND ISLAND DRESSING

2 c. homemade Miracle Whip	1/4 c. oil
1/2 c. honey	1/2 c. vinegar
1/2 c. catsup	dash of red pepper, paprika,
1/4 t. salt	and garlic salt

Combine all ingredients in bowl and beat together until smooth.

SALADS AND DRESSINGS

Sesame seeds improve a salad.

COLESLAW DRESSING▾

4 T. yogurt	1 t. lemon juice
1 T. olive oil	2 T. fresh dill, cut fine

Mix with shredded cabbage and place parsley sprigs on top.

FRUIT DIP▾

1 c. yogurt cream cheese or yogurt or 1/2 and 1/2
orange juice or pineapple juice as desired
1 c. whipped cream, folded in
vanilla flavoring (optional)

Mix altogether.

HEALTHY VEGETABLE DIP▾

1 c. yogurt (part yogurt cream cheese may be used)

Add minced onions - about 1 T., and a little soy sauce. A little parsley, chives, or sesame seeds could be added. A packet of onion soup mix from the health food store may be added.

PAPRIKA DIP

1 c. yogurt	1 T. basil
1/4 c. homemade Miracle Whip (pg. 86)	1/2 t. chili powder
	sea salt to taste
1 t. paprika	

Combine all ingredients. Chill and serve.

PINEAPPLE DIP

1/2 c. cream cheese

2 T. crushed pineapple

1/2 c. finely chopped dates

1/2 c. shredded coconut

Mix well and chill. Spread on crackers or fill celery.

TOMATO DIP

3/4 c. yogurt

1 T. onion flakes

1/4 t. mustard

1/3 c. catsup

1 1/4 c. cottage cheese

1 t. lemon juice

1 t. soy sauce

Sieve cottage cheese and fold in the rest of the ingredients.

VEGETABLE DIP

1 c. sour cream

1 T. parsley flakes

1/2 t. onion salt

1 c. Miracle Whip

1/2 t. garlic salt

Combine all ingredients, mix together. Chill and serve.

SALADS AND DRESSINGS

When growing your own sprouts be careful to avoid treated seeds.

COTTAGE CHEESE SALAD

2 T. gelatin   1 c. boiling water
1/4 c. cold water   1 c. cold water or fruit juice
6 oz. frozen orange juice

Soften gelatin in cold water. Then pour boiling water over gelatin and stir until dissolved. Add cold water or fruit juice and frozen orange juice. As juice melts, gelatin will become thick.

When partially set, beat in the following:
1 lb. cottage cheese
1 can drained, crushed, unsweetened pineapple
1 c. cream, whipped, with vanilla and honey added
nuts

Variation: Add 2 cups of fruit instead of the cottage cheese mixture.

cookies

COOKIES

CARROT OATMEAL COOKIES

Cream:

1/2 c. butter	1/2 c. maple syrup

Add:

2 beaten eggs	1/3 c. milk
1 1/2 c. grated carrots	

Sift, then add:

2 c. whole wheat flour	1/4 t. salt
1 t. baking powder	1/4 t. cinnamon
1/4 t. baking soda	1/4 t. nutmeg

Mix well and add:

1 c. rolled oats	1 c. raisins

Bake 15 minutes at 350°.

OATMEAL FRUIT COOKIES▼

1 c. sifted flour	1/4 t. cloves
1/2 t. cinnamon	1 t. baking soda

Sift together.

1 c. apple juice	1/2 c. chopped dates
1/2 c. chopped apples	1/2 c. raisins
1/2 c. butter	1 c. oatmeal

Bring juice, dates, apples, butter, raisins, and oatmeal to a boil. Simmer 3 min. Remove from heat and stir into dry mixture until well blended. Cool. Cover and refrigerate overnight. Drop by teaspoonful, 2 in. apart, on a greased baking sheet. Bake at 350° for 10 - 14 min.

WHEAT AND OATMEAL COOKIES *too much flour*

3 c. honey	10½ c. whole wheat flour
1 c. cane molasses	20 c. oatmeal
5 c. oil	4 t. salt
16 eggs	4 t. baking soda
4 T. vanilla	4 t. baking powder

Beat eggs, add oil, honey, molasses, and vanilla. Beat well then add rest of ingredients. Drop onto cookie sheet and bake at 350° until golden.

GRANOLA COOKIES

Mix well:

1 beaten egg	1/3 c. oil
1/3 c. honey	1/2 t. vanilla

Then add:

1 c. whole wheat flour	1/2 t. baking soda
1/2 t. sea salt	1 1/4 c. granola

Mix thoroughly and bake for 10 minutes at 325°.

PEANUT BUTTER COOKIES

3/4 c. butter	3 t. cinnamon
1 c. honey	3 c. wheat flour
2 eggs	3 t. baking soda
2 t. vanilla	1 t. salt
1 c. peanut butter	1/2 t. nutmeg

Thoroughly cream butter, honey, eggs, and vanilla. Stir in peanut butter. Sift dry ingredients and stir into creamed mixture. Drop by teaspoon onto cookie sheets. Flatten with a fork or the flat bottom of a cup. Bake at 350° for 10 minutes. Very good.

COOKIES

Use only pure vanilla. The imitation kinds have chemicals.

COOKIES

SOUR CREAM COOKIES

1/2 c. butter	2 t. baking soda
1 c. honey	3 1/2 c. wheat flour
2 or 3 eggs	2 t. baking powder
2 t. vanilla	1/2 t. salt
2 t. lemon flavoring	2 t. cinnamon
1 c. thick, sour, cream	

Mix butter and honey. Add eggs and flavorings and beat until smooth. Dissolve baking soda in cream. Mix dry ingredients together with cream. Stir until stiff drop batter is formed. Drop by teaspoon onto a greased cookie sheet. Bake 7 minutes at 350°. Makes 6 doz.

SORGHUM COOKIES

Mix and beat until fluffy:

2 c. sorghum	3 t. baking soda

Then add:

1 c. olive oil	3 eggs
2 c. oatmeal	1 t. vanilla

Enough whole wheat flour to make a soft dough. Bake at 400°.

SORGHUM COOKIES

1/2 gal. sorghum	2 lbs. butter
1 qt. buttermilk	1 T. salt
1/2 c. baking soda (scant)	2 T. nutmeg
1 qt. chopped nuts	2 T. cinnamon
5 lbs. + 4 cups whole wheat flour	
2 lbs. raisins	

Roll dough into balls and flatten on cookie sheets. Bake at 325° - 350° until they flatten and are nice and brown, but not burnt. This recipe makes 200 - 300 cookies, depending on the size.

Note: The older they get, the better. Make in October to serve at Christmas.

MOLASSES COOKIES

2 c. oil	1 T. ginger
3 c. molasses	1 T. cinnamon
1 t. salt	1 c. water
2 T. baking soda	8 c. wheat flour

Chill dough for several hours. Roll 1/4 in. thick. Cut in a round shape. Glaze with beaten egg. Bake for 10 min. This is a soft cookie.

Note: When storing, put plastic or Saran Wrap between layers to keep cookies from sticking together.

COOKIES

To keep cookies soft, put a slice of bread in cookie container.

COOKIES

Make quick oats finer by putting them through a small meal grinder, and you have oat flour. Most any cake or cookie recipe can use some oat flour.

APPLESAUCE COOKIES

Stir until creamy:

1 c. honey	1/2 c. canola oil

Add:

2 beaten eggs	1 c. applesauce

Sift together and add:

2 1/2 c. stirred whole wheat flour

1/2 t. salt	1/2 t. baking powder
1 t. baking soda	1 t. cinnamon

Mix thoroughly and add:

1/2 t. vanilla	1 c. sunflower seeds

Drop by teaspoons onto greased cookie sheets and bake at 375° for 10 minutes.

NO-SUGAR COOKIES

Mix:

2 c. all bran	2 c. walnuts
1 c. wheat germ	4 t. baking powder
1 c. wheat flour	1 T. cinnamon
1 c. rolled oats	1 t. salt
1 c. whole almonds	1 c. raisins

Then add:

2 c. water	2 eggs, beaten
1 c. powdered milk	1 T. vanilla

Fold in:

5 bananas	4 T. honey
1/2 c. melted butter	

Bake at 350°.

SUGARLESS COOKIES

1/2 c. chopped apples	1 c. raisins
1/2 c. chopped dates	1 c. water

   Boil together 3 min. and cool.
   Add:

1 1/3 c. wheat flour	1 t. baking soda
1/3 c. oil	1 t. nutmeg (optional)
3 eggs	1 t. vanilla
1/3 c. chopped nuts	1/2 t. salt

   Mix well. Chill 15 min. Drop onto greased cookie sheet and bake.
   Note: These are best if baked fresh every meal.

COOKIES

PUMPKIN COOKIES

1/2 c. butter	2 c. cooked, mashed pumpkin
1/2 c. honey	1/4 c. molasses
3 c. wheat flour	2 eggs
1 1/2 c. rolled oats	3 t. vanilla
2 t. baking powder	3/4 t. salt
3 t. cinnamon	2 t. baking soda
1 T. vinegar	1/2 t. nutmeg
1 c. raisins	1/2 t. allspice

   Cream butter, honey, and molasses. Add eggs and vanilla. Mix dry ingredients together and add alternately with pumpkin. Last, add raisins and mix thoroughly. Drop by teaspoons onto lightly greased cookie sheet. Bake at 350°. May be iced if you wish.

COOKIES

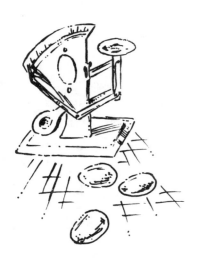

GINGER COOKIES

1/2 c. soft butter	3 t. ground ginger
1 c. honey	3 3/4 c. wheat flour
2 eggs, beaten	2 t. baking soda
1/4 c. molasses	2 t. cinnamon
2 t. vinegar	1/2 t. cloves

Cream butter and honey together. Stir in eggs, molasses, and vinegar. Sift and add dry ingredients. Drop by teaspoon onto greased cookie sheets. Flatten by dipping a glass in water and pressing cookie. Bake at 350°, watching closely so they don't get too hard. Makes 4 doz.

GINGERSNAPS

2 c. molasses	4 c. wheat flour
1 c. butter	3 t. baking soda
2 beaten eggs	1 t. cinnamon
1 t. vanilla	1 t. salt
2 t. baking powder	2 t. ginger

Cream butter and molasses. Add eggs, vanilla, and sifted dry ingredients. Chill until dough is cold (preferably ice-cold). I like to set my dough on ice. Roll into small balls and bake in moderately hot oven for 10 - 15 minutes.

SANDWICH COOKIES

2 c. butter	1/4 c. sorghum
1 c. honey	4 t. baking soda
3 eggs	2 t. lemon juice

enough wheat flour to roll thin

Roll dough and cut into small circles. Bake in moderately hot oven. When cooled, sandwich with jam, apple butter, or cooked dates. Store in tight container several days before using.

WHOOPIE PIE COOKIES

1 c. butter	4 c. wheat flour
1 1/3 c. sorghum	1 c. carob
2 eggs	2 t. salt
1 c. sour milk	2 t. baking soda
1 c. hot water	2 t. cinnamon
2 t. vanilla	

Cream together butter, sorghum, eggs, and vanilla. Sift together dry ingredients and add alternately with sour milk and hot water. If desired, you may use only 1/2 c. carob and substitute flour for the other half. Drop by teaspoon onto cookie sheet. Bake at 350° until done.

Cool. Spread bottom side of half the cookies with a layer of sorghum and peanut butter. Or you may use Butter Cream Frosting or something like it.

WHOOPIE PIES

Cream together:

1 c. honey	1/2 c. canola oil
1/2 t. salt	2 t. vanilla
2 eggs	

Then add:

2 c. rye flour	1/4 c. whole wheat flour
2 t. baking soda	1/4 c. carob powder
1 c. sour milk	

Drop by teaspoonfuls onto greased cookie sheet and bake at 400°. Spread cream cheese frosting between 2 cookies.

COOKIES

When your recipe calls for oil, use only the cold-pressed.

COOKIES

MAPLE BARS

Make a sponge of:

1 1/4 c. warm water	1 1/2 T. yeast
1/2 c. oil	1 t. salt
2 eggs	1/3 c. honey
3 c. whole wheat flour	

After this has risen, knead in 1 1/2 c. more of whole wheat flour. This will be a very sticky dough. Let rise.

Roll or pat dough into 2 cookie pans, putting oil on hands if needed to keep from sticking. Bake 10 min.

Ice with frosting into which maple flavoring has been added.

MINCEMEAT BARS

3 c. wheat flour	1/3 c. honey
2 c. oatmeal	1 t. salt
3/4 c. butter	1/2 t. baking soda

Mix to crumbs. Pat 3/4 of the crumbs in bottom of 13x9x2 cake pan. Spread on 6 c. mincemeat pie filling. Sprinkle remaining crumbs evenly on top. Pat gently until smooth. Bake until nicely browned.

OATMEAL BARS (UNSWEETENED) ▼

1/2 c. water
1/2 c. oil
1 1/2 c. carrots, butternut squash, or red beets, shredded
1/2 c. raisins or dates
  Mix well and add:
1 c. whole wheat flour
2 c. regular rolled oats
   (some bran or wheat germ may be used instead of oats)
1/2 - 1 c. nuts or sunflower seeds (optional)

1 t. vanilla
1/2 t. cinnamon (optional)

  Press into cake pan and bake 30 min. at 350°. Cut when hot and let cool before removing from pan.

COOKIES

OATMEAL COCONUT BARS

4 c. whole wheat flour
3 c. oatmeal
1 c. coconut
1 c. bran
  Stir together.
1 c. honey
1 T. blackstrap molasses

1 t. salt
1 t. baking soda
1/4 t. cinnamon

1/3 c. oil
2 eggs

  Blend into above well. Press into 1 or 2 greased bread pans (depending on how thick you want them). Chill 24 hrs., then knock out of pans. Slice and bake on cookie sheets at 345° for 22 minutes.

COOKIES

Grating a stick of butter softens it quickly.

PEANUT BUTTER BARS

2 c. whole wheat flour	1 c. wheat bran
2 c. oat bran	
Stir.	
1 1/4 t. salt	1 c. peanut butter
Stir together.	
1 c. sorghum	1/2 c. apple butter or sauce
2 T. vanilla	

Stir both mixtures and the last three ingredients together well. Press dough onto cookie sheet. Bake at 350° for 30 min. and cut while still warm.

TOASTED OAT BARS

4 c. quick oats	1 t. salt
1 1/2 c. chopped nuts	1 t. vanilla
3/4 c. melted butter	1 c. honey

Combine all ingredients. Mix well. Press firmly into well greased 15 1/2 x 10 1/2 in. pan. Bake at 350° for 12 min. or until golden brown. Let cool, then cut into bars.

FUDGE NUT BARS

1 c. butter	2 eggs
1 1/3 c. sorghum	2 t. vanilla

2 1/2 c. wheat flour, sifted before measuring

1 t. baking soda	1 t. salt

3 c. rolled oats

Cream together butter and sorghum. Beat in eggs and vanilla. Sift and add flour, soda, and salt. Stir in rolled oats. Set aside while you prepare filling.

3/4 c. carob powder	3/4 c. milk
2 t. cinnamon	1/2 t. salt
2 t. vanilla	3 T. butter

1/2 - 2/3 c. sorghum or maple syrup

1 c. chopped nuts

Blend together over low heat. Stir constantly, just until mixture comes to a slight boil.

Spread 2/3 of oatmeal mixture evenly in large jelly roll pan. Cover with filling. Dot with remaining dough and swirl it over filling. Bake at 350° for 25 - 30 min. or until lightly browned.

Note: Fudge Nut Filling is also good used as an ice cream topping, etc. Or use your favorite cream pie recipe and blend with Fudge Nut Filling until desired taste is reached. Top with whipped cream, drizzle with Fudge Nut Topping, and sprinkle with walnuts.

COOKIES

Before measuring honey or other syrup, oil the cup with cooking oil and rinse in hot water.

COOKIES

If you wish to use carob chips instead of chocolate chips, check the label. It may be 50 percent sugar.

DELICIOUS HEALTH BARS

In kettle, melt 3/4 c. butter, then add:

1/4 c. honey	5 eggs
1 c. molasses	1 t. vanilla

Beat well, then add all these ingredients before stirring:

1 c. flour	1 c. coconut
1 c. wheat germ	1 c. raisins
1 t. baking powder	1/2 c. nuts

Fold together in about 30 strokes. Bake in 9 x 13 pan at 350° for 30 min. Cut while warm.

NUTRITION BARS

Combine:

1 c. soft butter	1/2 c. honey
2 eggs	1 t. vanilla

Add:

1 1/2 c. whole wheat flour	1/2 t. salt
1/2 t. baking soda	1/2 c. carob chips
1 c. oatmeal	1/2 c. coconut
1/4 c. nutmeats	

Press into pan and bake. Let cool and eat in bars. Delicious with canned peaches.

HI-PROTEIN ENERGY BARS

1/2 c. butter	2 c. carob chips
5/8 c. honey	1/2 c. raisins
2 eggs	1 t. vanilla
1/3 c. carob powder	1/4 c. milk
1/4 c. nonfat dry milk	1/4 c. wheat germ
1 c. whole wheat flour	1/4 t. baking soda
1/2 t. baking powder	

Cream butter, honey, eggs, and vanilla until light and fluffy. Blend in carob powder and milk; add dry milk, wheat germ, flour, baking powder, and baking soda. Beat until ingredients are thoroughly combined. Fold in chips and raisins. Spread mixture in a greased 13x9x2 inch baking pan. Bake at 350° for 30 - 35 minutes. Cool. Cut into bars.

COOKIES

GRANOLA BARS (UNSWEETENED)▾

3 1/2 c. oatmeal (regular or mixed)
1 1/2 c. carrots, squash, or beets, shredded

1 egg	1/4 c. (or a little more) water
1/4 t. cinnamon	1 t. vanilla
1/2 c. oil	3/4 c. raisins or dates
3/4 c. nuts or sunflower seeds	

Mix thoroughly and press into regular size cake pan. Bake 20 min. at 350°. Cut when hot and let cool.

COOKIES

GREAT GRANOLA BARS

3 1/2 c. quick rolled oats
1/2 c. extra fine coconut
3/4 c. chopped walnuts
1 c. chopped dates
2/3 c. melted butter
1/3 c. honey

1/3 c. cane molasses
1 egg
1/2 t. cinnamon
1 t. vanilla
1/2 t. salt

Melt butter, remove from heat, and stir in honey, vanilla, and molasses. Add egg to the rest of the dry ingredients, then add butter mixture. Mix well and press into 13 x 9 pan. Bake at 350° for 20 min. Cut these when cool and remove from pan when completely cooled.

BLUEBERRY SNACKING BARS

1 7/8 c. wheat flour
1 c. milk
1/2 c. honey
2/3 c. oil
2 1/2 t. baking powder
2 t. cinnamon

2 t. vanilla
3/4 t. salt
3 eggs
3 c. blueberries
1 c. nuts

Mix together first 9 ingredients. Fold in nuts and blueberries. Bake at 350° for 45 min. or until done. Cut into bars.

RAISIN BARS

Cook 2 lbs. raisins in as little water as possible, and cool.
Mix:

6 c. whole wheat flour	2 c. shortening
5 c. quick rolled oats	1 t. salt
1 1/2 c. maple syrup	

Add the raisins, 5 beaten eggs, and 1 pt. molasses.

Pour 1/2 c. boiling water over 3 T. baking soda. Mix thoroughly with above. Chill dough overnight.

Form into rolls the length of a cookie sheet 1/2 inch thick.

Beat one egg and add a little milk, then spread on top.

Bake at 350°. Cool and cut.

DANISH APPLE BARS▾

Find the Delicious Whole Wheat Pastry Crust recipe under Desserts on page 129 and the Cider Snitz recipe under Breakfasts on page 34.

Take a little over 1/2 of the Pastry Crust and cover the bottom of a cookie sheet. Pour 4 - 5 cups of the snitz mixture on top. Roll out the remaining dough and place on top. Seal edges and brush top with beaten egg whites. Cut slits in the top for vents. Bake at 350° for 45 minutes or until done.

RAISIN CRISP

1 3/4 c. oatmeal	1/2 c. honey
1 3/4 c. whole wheat flour	3/4 c. melted butter

Mix together and press half of crumbs in a cake pan. Put raisin filling on top, then the rest of the crumbs. Bake 3/4 hour or until nice and brown. Cut into squares.

Raisin Filling:

Cook 2 c. raisins and 2 c. water together. Thicken with 2 level T. corn or potato starch. Remove from heat and add 2 T. lemon juice.

When baking cookies, press a carob chip in the center of each cookie as soon as you take them out of the oven. The heat from the cookie melts the chip enough for it to stick to the cookie.

COOKIES

Soften butter for spreading by inverting a small heated pan over the butter dish.

CAROB SQUARES

1/2 c. butter	1/2 c. coconut
1/2 c. honey	1/2 c. chopped nuts
1/4 c. carob powder	1/2 c. graham crackers, crushed
2 eggs, separated	1/8 t. vanilla

Line 8 x 8 pan with graham crackers, or bake your favorite cookie recipe in pan for bottom. Make cookie layer very thin. Melt butter in heavy skillet. Combine honey, carob powder, and egg yolks. Cook until partly thickened. Add vanilla, crushed wafers, and coconut. Beat egg whites until stiff and fold in last. Allow to stand in fridge overnight. Sprinkle with coconut or ice with your favorite icing.

CAROB BROWNIES▾

1 1/2 c. whole wheat flour	1/2 c. carob powder
1 t. salt	1 c. canola oil
4 eggs	2 t. vanilla
1/2 c. nuts	1/2 c. unsweetened coconut

Mix all ingredients except nuts and coconut in bowl. Beat 3 minutes. If batter seems stiff, add some water or cider. Place in 10 x 13 cake pan or into cupcake liners. Sprinkle nuts and coconut on top. Bake at 350° for 20 - 25 minutes.

Note: When yeast is under control, you may add some apple juice concentrate for some of the liquid.

MATRIMONY SQUARES

Crumbs:

2 c. oatmeal
2 c. wheat flour
1 c. butter
1/2 c. honey
1/2 t. salt

Filling:

3 c. dates
1/2 c. honey
1 t. vanilla
water to cover

Cook filling until well thickened. Set aside to cool. Mix crumbs. Press 3/4 of crumbs into bottom of 9 x 13 cake pan. Spread filling on top of crumbs. Sprinkle remaining crumbs on top. Bake until nicely browned.

Note: 1 1/2 qt. well thickened and sweetened cooked fruit may be used instead of dates. Blueberries are our favorite.

MOM'S DELIGHT (LIKE BROWNIES)

3 c. wheat flour
1/4 c. carob
1/2 t. cinnamon
1/2 c. ground, black walnuts
Stir.
1 1/2 c. water
1/2 c. honey
1/2 c. blackstrap molasses

1 c. bran
1 t. baking soda
1/2 t. salt

1/2 c. sunflower seeds
1 t. vanilla

Blend well and stir into above mixture. Pour into a greased 9 x 9 in. pan. Bake at 350° for 55 minutes.

COOKIES

114

COOKIES

CINNAMON ZUCCHINI BROWNIES

1/4 c. butter	3 t. cinnamon
1/2 c. honey	1 1/2 t. baking powder
1 egg	1/2 t. salt
2 t. vanilla	1/2 t. nutmeg
1 c. wheat flour	1 c. grated zucchini
1/2 c. chopped nuts (optional)	

Mix butter and honey. Add egg and vanilla and beat well. Add mixed dry ingredients and stir. Add zucchini and nuts. Bake in greased 9 x 9 in. pan at 350° for 25 minutes.

BANANA CUPCAKES

6 T. butter	3/4 t. salt
1/2 c. honey	1 t. cinnamon
2 eggs	1 t. baking soda dissolved
2 t. vanilla	in 1 T. water
1 1/2 c. wheat flour	1/4 t. allspice
1 1/4 t. baking powder	1 c. mashed bananas

Cream butter and honey together. Add eggs and vanilla and beat. Sift dry ingredients together and add alternately with water and baking soda and banana pulp. Mix thoroughly and fill greased cupcake or muffin tins 2/3 full. Bake at 350° for 25 minutes. Makes 16 - 18 cupcakes. Delicious!

FIG BRAID

Dough:

1 1/2 c. whole wheat flour	1 t. salt
1 1/2 T. yeast	

Stir together.

1/2 c. honey	1/3 c. oil
1/4 c. warm water	

Beat into above.

2 eggs	1 1/2 c. whole wheat flour

Beat into above about 2 minutes.

3 c. whole wheat flour

Gradually add to above. Knead, then let rest 15 minutes. Cut into 3 equal pieces. Roll each piece out to 12 in. x 17 in. Place on a greased tray. Fill center of each piece with equal amounts of filling. Cut 1 in. wide strips on each side of filling. Fold strips back and forth across filling. Sprinkle topping on top of each roll. Cover and let rise 1 - 1 1/2 hours until double. Bake at 375° for 20 - 25 minutes.

Filling:

2 1/4 c. dried fruit	1 1/2 c. water

Simmer until liquid is absorbed and fruit is tender, about 20 minutes. Pureé. Add honey only if desired.

Crumb Topping:

3/4 c. whole wheat flour	2 T. oil
3/4 t. cinnamon	2 T. honey

Mix until crumbly.

COOKIES

A dip of the spoon or cup into hot water before measuring shortening or butter will cause the fat to slip out easily without sticking to the spoon.

116

NOTES

cakes

CAKES

Is your cake heavy or stale? Cut it up and pour a pudding or lemon sauce over it.

MARBLE CAKE

White part:

1/2 c. butter	3/4 c. milk
1/2 c. honey	4 egg whites
2 1/2 c. whole wheat flour	2 t. vanilla
2 1/2 t. baking powder	2 t. cinnamon
1/2 t. salt	

Cream butter and honey together. Add vanilla and beat, then sift dry ingredients together and add alternately with milk. Mix thoroughly. Fold in stiffly beaten egg whites.

Dark part:

1/2 c. butter	1 1/2 t. baking soda
1/2 c. honey	1/2 t. salt
4 egg yolks	2 t. cinnamon
1/3 c. molasses	1 1/2 t. cloves
1/4 c. carob powder	1 1/2 t. nutmeg
2 c. whole wheat flour	1 1/4 c. sour milk

Cream butter and honey together, add molasses and egg yolks, and blend thoroughly. Sift dry ingredients together and add alternately with milk. Beat thoroughly.

Drop alternate spoonfuls of each batter into greased tube pan to make a marbled effect. Bake at 350° for 1 hour.

ROLLED OATS CAKE

1 1/2 c. boiling water over 1 c. oats
1/2 c. butter

Let cool and add:

1 c. maple syrup	1 t. cinnamon
1 1/2 c. whole wheat flour	1 t. baking soda

Bake in small loaf pan for 30 minutes at 350°.

CAROB OATMEAL CAKE

1 c. oatmeal   1/4 c. carob powder

Pour 1 1/2 c. boiling water over this and stir until smooth. Let cool.
Mix separately:

1 c. maple syrup   1/2 c. oil (scant)

2 beaten eggs   1 t. vanilla

1/4 t. salt   1 t. baking soda

1 c. whole wheat flour

Cream oil and syrup. Add baking soda, salt, and flour. Then add eggs, vanilla, and carob mixture. Stir well.

Bake at 350° for 45 minutes. Top with coconut and sunflower seeds before baking if you wish.

SPICE OATMEAL CAKE

1 c. rolled oats   2 t. baking soda

1 1/4 c. boiling water   1 t. salt

1 stick (1/2 cup) butter   4 t. cinnamon

1 1/2 c. honey   1 3/4 c. wheat flour

2 t. vanilla   2 t. nutmeg

3 eggs, beaten   2 t. cloves

Place oats, butter, and boiling water in large bowl and let sit for 20 minutes. Add honey, vanilla, and eggs, Mix together rest of ingredients and add to above. Pour into a greased and floured 9 x 13 inch cake pan. Bake 30 - 40 minutes at 350°.

Note: This cake freezes well.

When changing a recipe from white flour to whole grain flour, double the spices, or sometimes triple them. Whole grain baked items tend to be more bland and spices are rich in trace elements. Use them generously.

CAKES

GERMAN CRUMB CAKE

Sift:

2 c. wheat flour	2 t. nutmeg
1/2 t. salt	2 t. ground cloves
3 t. cinnamon	

Mix with 6 T. butter and 1/2 c. honey. Remove 1/2 c. of crumbs and save for topping.

Mix with the remaining crumbs:

1 egg	1 c. sour milk
2 T. molasses	2 t. baking soda

Pour into greased pan and top with remaining crumbs. Bake 45 minutes at 350°.

CAROB BLACK CRACK CAKE

3 c. wheat flour	1 c. oat bran
1 c. wheat bran	1 c. coconut
1 c. cornmeal	1 c. raisins

Stir.

1/4 c. oil	2/3 c. blackstrap molasses
1/2 c. honey	2/3 c. carob powder
2 c. water	1/4 t. cloves
1/2 t. salt	3/4 t. baking soda
1/2 t. cinnamon	

Blend and stir into first mixture. Pour into a greased 8 x 11 1/2 x 2 inch pan. Bake at 350° for 45 minutes.

Variations: Make into drop cookies. Drop onto trays. Bake at 350° for 15 minutets.

Make the following changes:

1/2 c. toasted coconut	1/2 c. blackstrap molasses
2 T. oil	1/2 c. carob powder
2/3 c. peanut butter	

Press into 3 bread pans. Chill and slice. Bake at 325° for 20 minutes.

CAROB POTATO CAKE

1/2 c. honey	pinch of nutmeg and salt
2 eggs, well beaten	1/3 c. buttermilk
1/2 c. cold mashed potatoes	1/2 c. oil
1 c. wheat flour	1/2 t. cinnamon
1/3 c. carob powder	1/2 t. baking soda
1 t. baking powder	

Beat honey and oil together. Add eggs and mashed potatoes. Beat with rotary beater. Blend in sifted dry ingredients and buttermilk. Beat well. Bake in 8 inch square pan.

PEANUT BUTTER BRAN CAKE

3 1/2 c. wheat flour	1 1/2 c. wheat bran
1/2 c. cornmeal	1 c. raisins
Stir.	
2 c. water	1 c. sorghum
1/2 t. baking soda	3/4 t. salt
1 c. peanut butter	

Blend until smooth. Stir into above. Pour into an 8 x 11 1/2 x 2 1/2 pan. Bake at 350° for 55 minutes.

Variation: Omit baking soda; use 1 t. salt. Heat all liquids, stir in 1 T. yeast. Let set to sponge, then stir into dry ingredients. Put large mounds on trays. Let rise 30 minutes. Bake at 350° for 30 - 35 minutes.

CAKES

When measuring flour, stir or fluff it up first. This helps give baked items a lighter texture.

CAKES

Set out eggs at least an hour before making a cake. If eggs are at room temperature, the cake will be lighter and fluffier.

PUMPKIN CAKE

1 1/2 c. wheat flour	1 t. baking soda
2 t. baking powder	1/2 t. salt
1 t. cinnamon	1/2 t. nutmeg
1/4 t. ginger	1/4 t. cloves
3/4 c. honey	1/2 c. oil
2/3 c. water or milk	2 eggs
1 c. cooked pumpkin	

Beat eggs, add oil and other ingredients except the flour. Beat well then blend in flour. Pour into greased cake pan and bake at 350° until golden.

COFFEE CAKE

1 1/2 c. wheat flour	3/4 c. milk
1/2 c. honey (scant)	1 egg
2 1/2 t. baking powder	3/4 t. salt
6 T. butter	1 t. vanilla
1 t. cinnamon	

Combine all ingredients and beat one half minute. Spread half of batter in greased square pan. Sprinkle half of topping (below) over batter. Pour remaining batter on top, then rest of batter. Bake at 375°.

Topping:

1/4 c. honey	2 t. cinnamon
2 T. melted butter	1/2 c. chopped nuts

Combine all ingredients.

LEMON PUDDING CAKE

4 eggs, separated
1/3 c. lemon juice
1 T. melted butter
3/4 c. honey, slightly warmed
2/3 c. whole wheat flour
1/2 t. salt
1 1/2 c. milk

Beat together the egg yolks, lemon juice, and butter until thick. Combine flour and salt and add to egg mixture with milk, beating until smooth. Beat egg whites until frothy. Add honey gradually, beating until firm, yet soft peaks form. Blend into batter. Pour into 8" square baking dish. Set in pan of hot water to bake. Bake at 350° for about 45 minutes or until golden brown. Serve warm. May be topped with whipped cream (delicious with peaches). Makes 8 or 9 servings.

SPICY GRANOLA CAKE

Mix:
3 c. finely ground wheat
3 c. oatmeal
3/4 c. honey
1 c. butter
3 t. allspice
2 t. baking soda
1 t. salt

After setting aside 2 c. of these crumbs, add to rest of mixture:
2 c. sour milk
3 eggs
vanilla to taste

Mix well and put in pan. Top with 2 c. of crumbs and bake.

CAKES

CAKES

If you have a recipe asking for white flour and you wish to substitute whole grains, use this table:

1 c. white flour =

3/4 c. whole wheat flour

7/8 c. rice flour

1/4 c. rye flour

5/8 c. potato flour

3/4 c. buckwheat flour

7/8 c. cornmeal

1 1/2 c. oatmeal

AUTUMN SURPRISE CAKE

2 c. unpeeled, diced apples
3/4 c. honey
1 1/2 c. whole wheat flour
1 1/2 t. baking soda
1/2 t. salt
1/2 c. chopped nuts
1 t. vanilla
1 egg, beaten
1/2 c. oil
1 c. coconut

Mix apples and honey. Sift flour, salt, and soda together. Add apples and remaining ingredients and mix thoroughly. Pour into greased, floured, 8 inch square pan and bake at 350° for 40 - 45 minutes.

ZUCCHINI FUDGE CAKE

4 eggs
2 t. vanilla
3 c. whole wheat flour
2 t. cinnamon
1 t. baking soda
1 c. buttermilk
3 c. shredded, unpeeled zucchini
3/4 c. maple syrup
3/4 t. butter or oil
1/2 c. carob powder
2 t. baking powder
3/4 t. salt
1 c. chopped walnuts

In a large bowl, beat eggs until fluffy. Add syrup gradually, beating well. Beat in vanilla and butter. Combine flour, carob, cinnamon, baking powder, baking soda, and salt. Stir 1/2 of dry ingredients into egg mixture. Add buttermilk; mix. Add remaining flour mixture; beat until smooth. Fold in zucchini and nuts. Pour batter into 13" x 9" pan. Bake at 350° for about 45 - 50 minutes or until top springs back when gently touched.

Variations: Nuts, seeds, or coconut may be sprinkled on top. If cocoa is used instead of carob, the cinnamon may be omitted.

MOIST BANANA FRUIT CAKE

Beat:

1/4 c. honey	4 eggs
1/2 c. molasses	1 c. butter
5 mashed bananas	1/2 c. jelly

Combine:

3 c. flour	3/4 t. nutmeg
3/4 t. cloves	1 1/2 t. cinnamon
1 t. baking soda	

Add last:

1 c. chopped dates	1 1/2 c. nuts
1 1/2 c. raisins	
1 c. colored fruit or cherries (optional)	

Bake at 275° for 2 1/2 - 3 hours. Keep a small pan of water in oven to keep the cake moist. Makes 1 tube pan or 3 - 4 loaf pans.

When cool, wrap in waxed paper, then tin foil, and put in plastic bags. Store in a cool dry place for 2 - 3 weeks.

FATHER'S CHOICE CAKE

2 c. raisins	4 T. butter
2 1/2 c. honey	2 t. cinnamon
3 c. water	pinch of allspice

Bring to a boil and simmer 15 minutes. Cool Sift together:

3 1/2 c. wheat flour	1/3 t. salt
1 t. baking soda	

Stir into above mixture. Bake 45 minutes or until done at 350°.

Note: I've used this for birthday cakes. Adding carob chips makes it good, too.

CAKES

Instead of using powdered sugar in icings, try non-instant powdered milk.

CAKES

MOLASSES CAKE

1 egg	1 t. cinnamon
1/2 c. honey	1/4 t. ginger
2 T. butter	1/4 t. salt
1/3 c. sorghum	1 1/2 c. graham flour
1/4 t. cloves	1 t. baking soda in 1 c. hot water

Bake at 350° - 375° for 40 - 50 minutes.

PINEAPPLE SHEET CAKE

2 c. whole wheat flour	2 eggs
1 c. maple syrup	2 t. baking soda
1/4 t. salt	1 t. vanilla
1/2 c. chopped nuts	1 - 20 oz. can crushed pineapple

Bake at 350° for 20 minutes. Frost with cream cheese frosting. Very good.

HONEY APPLESAUCE CAKE

1/2 c. oil	1/4 t. salt
1 c. honey	1 t. cinnamon
2 eggs	1 1/2 c. applesauce
3 c. whole wheat flour	1 c. raisins
1 1/2 t. baking soda	1/2 c. chopped nuts

Cream oil and honey until well mixed. Beat eggs into creamed mixture, adding one at a time and mixing well. Add dry ingredients alternately with the applesauce. Add nuts and raisins. Pour into well greased cake pan and bake at 325° for 40 minutes.

APPLESAUCE CAKE

3/4 c. honey or maple syrup
1/2 c. oil
1 egg
1 t. baking soda
1 t. nutmeg or allspice
   Fills a small cake pan.

1 c. raisins
1 c. flour
1 c. applesauce
1 t. cinnamon
1/4 c. nuts

APPLE CAKE

Mix and let stand for 1 hour:

4 c. diced apples
3/4 c. honey
2 t. vanilla (optional)
   Add:
2 beaten eggs
2 c. flour
1 c. chopped nuts
   Bake in greased and floured tube pan at 350° for 50 minutes.

1 c. oil
2 t. cinnamon
1/2 t. salt

1 t. baking soda
1 c. raisins

When mixing a recipe that calls for raisins, first simmer them in a little water and let cool a bit. This way your recipe will need less sweetener and liquid.

CAKES

PEAR SAUCE DELIGHT CAKE

4 c. wheat flour	1 c. bran
1/4 c. carob powder	1 1/2 t. baking soda
1 t. cinnamon	1/4 t. salt
1/4 t. cloves	3/4 c. raisins
1/2 c. roasted cornmeal	

   Stir altogether.

2 c. pear sauce or applesauce	1 t. vanilla
1 1/2 c. water	3/4 c. honey

   Blend and stir into above. Pour into a greased 9 x 13 pan. Bake at 350°
for 50 minutes.

WHOLE WHEAT CHOCOLATE CAKE

3 c. wheat flour	1 1/2 c. honey
2/3 c. carob powder	1 1/4 c. mayonnaise
1 T. baking powder	1 1/4 c. water
1 1/2 t. baking soda	1 T. vanilla
1/2 t. salt	

   Combine first 5 ingredients. In a separate bowl, mix last 4 ingredients.
Gradually add to first mixture and stir until smooth. Bake in 13 x 9 inch pan
for 40 - 45 minutes at 350°.

NUTRITION CAKE

2 eggs	1/2 tsp. baking soda
1 t. vanilla	1/2 tsp. salt
1 c. soft butter	1 c. oatmeal
1/2 c. honey	1 c. coconut
1/2 c. whole wheat flour	

   Combine first 4 ingredients. Add last 5 and press into a greased 9" x 13"
pan. Bake at 350° for 20 - 25 minutes.

WACKY CAKE

1 3/4 c. wheat flour
1/4 t. salt
2 t. baking soda
1 3/4 T. carob
1 T. vinegar

1/2 c. oil
3/4 c. honey
1 1/2 t. vanilla
1 c. water

Sift dry ingredients into 8 x 8 inch pan. Mix oil and honey together. Make 3 holes in dry mixture. In one put the vinegar. In another put the vanilla. In the third pour the oil and honey mixture. Pour the water over the whole thing. Mix with a fork but do not beat. Bake at 350° until done.

PINEAPPLE CAKE

2 c. spelt flour
3/4 c. honey
2 tsp. baking soda
1 tsp. vanilla

1 20-oz. can crushed pineapple
  with juice
1 c. unsweetened coconut
1 c. nuts, chopped

Mix well and pour into buttered 9" x 13" cake pan. Bake at 350° for 45 min.

Topping:

3 - 4 oz. softened cream cheese
1/2 c. unsweetened coconut
maple syrup
vanilla

1/4 c. butter
1/2 c. nuts
powdered sugar

CAKES

Use a cast iron skillet to melt your butter, then bake your batter in it. The hot skillet does a good job of baking evenly and thoroughly.

CARROT CAKE

2 1/4 c. whole wheat flour
1 1/2 c. oatmeal soaked in   3/4 c. apple juice
2 t. baking powder   1 t. baking soda
1 1/2 t. cinnamon   1/3 c. canola oil
1 1/4 c. honey   4 eggs

Beat thoroughly several minutes. Add 2 c. grated carrots and 3/4 c. walnut pieces. Bake at 325° for 50 - 60 minutes.

CARROT CAKE

2 1/4 c. wheat flour   5 eggs, separated
2 t. baking powder   1 t. salt
3 t. cinnamon   1 t. nutmeg
1/4 t. ginger   3 t. baking soda
3 c. grated carrots   1 t. allspice
1 c. ground nuts (optional)   3/4 c. raisins
1 1/3 c. oil   1 c. honey

Sift dry ingredients together. Set aside. Mix grated carrots, raisins, and nuts. Set aside. Combine oil and honey and add to carrot mixture.

Separate eggs and beat yolks until frothy. Mix into cake mixture. Beat egg whites until very stiff. Fold carefully into cake mixture. Pour into greased tube pan or 2 loaf pans. Bake 1 hour at 350° or until done. Cool before cutting.

PINEAPPLE CARROT CAKE▾

1 c. dates   1 c. water
1 c. raisins

Chop and blend fruit. Then add water and boil 3 minutes. Add 1 stick butter. Stir and cool.

In a mixing bowl, blend date mixture with the following:

1 t. baking soda   2 eggs
1 t. vanilla

Mix well and add:

8 oz. unsweetened crushed pineapple
1 c. grated fresh coconut   1 c. chopped nuts
1/2 c. chopped carrots   2 c. flour

Pour into greased oblong pan. Bake at 375° for 25 minutes. When cool, it may be topped with frosting made of crushed pineapple mixed with softened cream cheese.

DOUBLE DELIGHT

3/4 c. oatmeal   1/4 c. raisins
1/4 c. honey   1 c. butter
2 t. baking powder   1/2 t. salt
1 c. carob chips   1 egg
1 c. flour

Combine all ingredients in bowl. Beat at low speed for 3 minutes, scraping sides of bowl often. Spread batter evenly in greased 10 x 15 pan. Bake at 350° for 25 - 30 minutes or until golden brown.

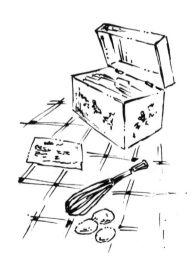

CAKES

BEST GINGERBREAD

1/2 c. butter	1 t. ginger
1/4 c. honey	1/2 t. cloves
1 egg, beaten	1/2 t. salt
1 1/2 t. baking soda	1 c. sorghum
1 t. cinnamon	1 c. hot water
2 1/2 c. sifted graham flour	

Preheat oven to 350°. Cream butter and honey. Add beaten egg. Measure and sift dry ingredients. Combine sorghum and hot water. Add dry ingredients to first mixture, alternately with sorghum, beating after each addition, until smooth. Line 9 x 9 x 2 inch pan with waxed paper and bake at 350° until done. Cut into squares and serve on individual plates, topped with whipped cream. Or eat hot with milk or lemon sauce.

GLORIFIED GINGERBREAD

Sift together into bowl:

4 c. wheat flour	1/2 t. salt
1 t. cinnamon	1 t. ginger

Add 1 c. butter.

Blend into fine crumbs. Set aside 3/4 of the mixture. To the ramainder, add:

1 1/4 c. sorghum	2 t. baking soda
2 eggs	1/4 t. salt
2 c. buttermilk or sour milk	

Pour batter into 9 x 13 inch pan. Sprinkle reserved crumbs over top, which have been mixed with a little honey if desired. Bake at 350° for 50 minutes or until done.

BANANA CHIFFON CAKE

1. Put dry ingredients in a bowl:

2 c. whole wheat flour	3 t. baking powder
1 t. salt	

2. Combine the following and add to above:

1/2 c. oil	3/4 c. honey
1/2 c. fruit juice	1 T. lemon juice
1 c. mashed bananas	7 egg yolks
vanilla and almond flavoring	

3. Beat the 7 egg whites and fold into batter. Pour into ungreased tube pan and bake. Invert and cool.

WHOLE WHEAT ANGEL FOOD CAKE

Beat together until stiff peaks form:

2 egg whites	1/4 t. salt
1 1/4 t. cream of tartar	vanilla to taste

Add in 3 - 4 additions:

1/3 c. each of honey, maple syrup, and sorghum

You may want to use a scraper to mix these in, as they tend to settle to the bottom of the bowl.

Sift together 5 times and add in several additions:

1/4 c. arrowroot or cornstarch powder

1 c. wheat flour	2 T. carob
1 t. cinnamon	dash of nutmeg

Pour batter into tube pan. Bake at 350° for 1 hour or until done.

CAKES

1 lemon = 3 – 4 T. lemon juice

1 orange = 6 – 8 T. orange juice

CAKES

Adding unsweetened applesauce or banana to cake or cookie dough will make it more moist. If you use small amounts (1/4 - 1/2 cup) you won't taste it.

ANGEL FOOD CAKE (WHOLE WHEAT AND HONEY)

2 1/3 c. egg whites	2 t. vanilla
1 t. salt	1/2 t. almond flavoring
2 t. cream of tartar	1/2 t. coconut flavoring

Have eggs at room temperature. Add the rest of the ingredients above. Beat until very soft peaks form. Gradually beat in 1 1/4 c. slightly warmed honey.

Sift over the beaten egg white mixture, in 4 additions, 1 3/4 c. sifted whole wheat flour. Fold each addition of flour over egg whites, carefully. Bake in tube pan at 350° for about 35 - 40 minutes.

STEAMED GRAHAM CAKE

2 c. whole wheat flour	1/2 c. nuts
1/4 c. honey	1 t. baking soda
1/4 c. molasses	1/2 t. cinnamon
1 egg	1/2 t. cloves
1/2 c. raisins	pinch of salt

Mix altogether. Leave batter in mixing bowl and set in a kettle of boiling water. Cover and steam for 1 hour and 15 minutes.

Eat hot with fruit and milk. A delicious supper.

FRUIT CAKE▾

1 c. dates	3 c. whole wheat flour
1 c. prunes	3 t. baking soda
1 c. raisins	2/3 c. butter
2 eggs	

Cook dates, prunes, raisins, and 2 c. water together. Cool and mix into flour and all other ingredients. Mix. Bake at 325° for 25 minutes or until done.

COCONUT ICING

2 c. unsweetened shredded coconut
1 c. wheat germ
5 T. honey
4 T. oil

Mix coconut and wheat germ. Mix oil and honey. Now mix them both together. Spread on cake. Delicious!

CAROB FROSTING

2 T. softened butter   2 T. warm honey
1/2 c. powdered milk   1 t. vanilla
1/4 c. carob powder

Beat in small bowl with fork, gradually adding a small amount of very hot water, while stirring until desired consistency is obtained. Immediately spread on cake.

Note: It works best to spread this frosting on cake while cake is still quite warm.

CAROB FUDGE FROSTING

1/2 c. honey   2 1/2 T. carob powder
1/3 c. milk   2 T. butter
2 t. vanilla

Combine honey, carob powder, and milk in a saucepan. Cook over medium heat to a soft ball stage (240°). Remove from heat. Add butter and vanilla. Allow to cool to lukewarm, then beat until thick.

CAKES

CREAM CHEESE FROSTING

Soften 4 oz. cream cheese. Beat until smooth and add 1/2 c. dry milk. Add 1 T. honey or sorghum and enough milk to make a spreading consistency.

For chocolate frosting, add a little carob powder. Sprinkle coconut on top (optional).

BANANA CREME FROSTING

4 oz. cream cheese   1/4 t. pure vanilla
1/4 c. softened butter   1 mashed banana
1/4 c. honey

Whip cream cheese and butter. Add vanilla and honey and whip 1 - 2 minutes until smooth. Fold in mashed banana and spread.

BUTTER CREAM FROSTING

3 T. (slightly rounded) cornstarch
1/3 - 1/2 c. maple syrup   1 c. milk

Blend together and boil until very thick, stirring constantly. Cool. Cream together:

1/3 - 1/2 c. butter   1 t. vanilla

Add to boiled mixture. Beat at high speed until fluffy.

Variation: Add crushed pineapple for Pineapple Butter Cream Frosting.

SUGAR FREE ICING

This recipe is good for decorating cakes!

1 pt. cream	1/2 t. vanilla
pinch of salt	

2 - 8 oz. pkgs. Philadelphia cream cheese at room temperature

Whip first three ingredients in chilled bowl. When it is thick enough to make peaks, add cream cheese and mix. You may add 1 T. or more non-instant milk powder to thicken for decorating.

SUGAR FREE ORANGE ICING▾

Combine:

2 T. soft butter	2 T. wheat flour

1/3 c. undiluted, frozen orange juice

Cook until thick. Beat in 3/4 - 1 c. milk powder or 4 oz. cream cheese.
Note: Milk powder will give your icing a glossy appearance.

ORANGE SYRUP

juice of 2 oranges	pinch of salt
3/8 c. honey	dash of cinnamon
4 T. lemon juice	

Boil 5 minutes. Pour over hot cake.

HONEY ICING

1/4 c. soft butter	1/2 c. honey
nuts or seeds	coconut

Blend together and spread over cake.

CAKES

For baking, it's best to use medium to large eggs; extra large eggs may cause cakes to fall when cooled.

CAKES

HONEY LEMON SAUCE

1/2 c. water	1 T. cornstarch
2 T. lemon juice	3 T. honey
1/2 t. salt	

Mix water, cornstarch, salt, and honey. Cook until thickened; add lemon juice. If desired, you may add slightly beaten egg yolk and cook slightly, stirring to prevent curdling. Remove from heat; add 1 t. butter. Best served warm. Makes 2/3 cup.

LEMON CAKE FILLING

3 T. cornstarch	1/4 c. honey
1/2 c. water	1 T. butter
1/4 c. lemon juice	

Cook over medium heat

FROSTING

1/2 c. honey	1/2 c. cream or milk
1/4 c. butter	

Boil 4 minutes, then add:

1/2 c. coconut	1/2 c. nuts

Spread over hot cake and brown in oven.

pies

PIES

CREAM CHEESE PIE

1 baked pie shell	8 oz. cream cheese
1 1/2 T. unflavored gelatin	1 c. yogurt
1/4 c. cold water	1/3 c. honey
2 eggs, beaten	2 t. vanilla
1/4 c. milk	

Mix gelatin and water and heat until gelatin dissolves. Blend eggs with milk and add to gelatin. Stirring constantly, cook over low heat until mixture coats a silver spoon. Cool. Cream honey, cheese, and vanilla. Add yogurt and continue mixing until smooth. Slowly stir in cold gelatin mixture. Chill a little more, then beat until creamy smooth. Pour into a nut or coconut pie shell. Refrigerate to set.

COCONUT CREAM PIE

1 baked pie shell	3 T. honey
8 oz. cream cheese	2 t. vanilla
1 c. yogurt	
1 1/4 c. shredded unsweetened coconut	

Blend together yogurt, cream cheese, honey, and vanilla. Fold in coconut, reserving a little for topping. Pour into pie shell. Top with remaining coconut and chill until set.

STRAWBERRY CREAM PIE

1 baked pie shell	1/4 c. honey
1 c. yogurt, drained	1 t. vanilla
8 oz. cream cheese	

2 c. sliced or cooked strawberries, sweetened

Combine yogurt, cream cheese, honey, and vanilla. Beat to the consistency of whipped cream. Pour into baked pie shell and refrigerate until set. Before serving, top with strawberries.

OR: Fold strawberries into cream pie before pouring into baked pie shell. Then pour into pie shell and refrigerate until set.

Variation: Use peaches, blueberries, or other sliced fruit instead of strawberries.

APPLE PIE▾

4 c. sliced apples	1/2 - 1 t. cinnamon
1/2 c. apple juice concentrate	1/2 - 1 t. nutmeg
2 t. flour	2 pie crusts
1/2 t. lemon juice	

Mix ingredients. Pour into prepared pie shell. Top with second crust. Bake at 425° for 40 - 45 minutes.

BLACKBERRY CUSTARD PIE

1 c. flour	1 c. honey
3 eggs (beat whites)	pinch of salt
3 c. milk	1/2 t. cinnamon

1/2 qt. blackberries or other fruit to each pie

Fold in beaten egg whites last. Sprinkle cinnamon on top. Makes 2 pies.

PIES

To avoid a soggy crust, brush bottom and sides with egg whites, sprinkle lightly with flour, and add the filling.

PIES

For golden brown pie crusts, brush top with cream before baking. Brushing with cold water makes it flaky.

CAROB PIE

1 c. raw cashews or almonds	1/2 c. carob powder
1/4 c. cornstarch	1/2 t. salt
1/4 c. dates	1/2 t. vanilla

Put all ingredients in blender, then add enough water to make 4 c. of liquid. Blend until smooth. Pour into pan and cook over medium heat, stirring occasionally, until mixture thickens. Pour into baked pie shell. Chill. Sprinkle coconut on top before serving.

PEACH AND PRALINE PIE

3 T. whole wheat flour	1/4 t. nutmeg
1/4 t. salt	3 eggs
1/2 c. maple syrup	

Combine and beat together well.

Stir in:

3 c. fresh peaches, cubed and peeled
   or 3 c. canned peaches, drained and cubed
1/4 c. butter, melted

Pour into pastry-lined pan.

Combine:

1/2 c. pecans, chopped	2 T. honey
1/3 c. wheat flour	2 T. soft butter

Sprinkle over top of filling. Bake at 400° for 35 - 45 minutes or until center is set.

HONEY PIE

1 c. honey
4 beaten eggs
1 c. chopped almonds
1 - 9 inch pie shell, unbaked

dash of nutmeg
dash of cinnamon
4 T. butter
2 t. vanilla

In a saucepan, bring honey to a boil. Add beaten eggs, stirring constantly with a fork. Add butter, vanilla, almonds, cinnamon, and nutmeg. Pour into pie shell and bake at 350° for 20 minutes or until filling is set.

OATMEAL PIE

3 beaten eggs
1/3 c. honey
1/2 c. molasses
2 T. browned butter
1/2 t. maple flavoring

1/4 c. quick oats
1/2 c. coconut
3/4 - 1 c. milk
1 t. vanilla
1/4 t. cinnamon

Blend together. Pour into unbaked pie shell. Bake 30 - 35 minutes at 350°.

PIES

PIES

Add 1 T. cider to raisin pie to improve taste.

PUMPKIN PIE

1 1/2 c. cooked pumpkin	1 1/4 c. milk
1/2 c. honey	1/2 t. salt
3 eggs, separated	1/4 t. ginger
2 T. cornstarch	1/4 t. cloves
1 t. cinnamon	pastry for 1 - 9 inch pie

Fold in stiffly beaten egg whites, at the last.

PUMPKIN PIE

4 eggs, separated	3 c. milk
2 c. mashed pumpkin	1/2 c. honey
1/4 c. wheat flour	1/2 c. sorghum
1/2 t. pumpkin pie spice	

Mix all ingredients except egg whites, beating thoroughly. Fold in stiffly beaten egg whites. Pour into 2 unbaked pie crusts. Bake in moderate oven until nicely browned and done.

IMPOSSIBLE PUMPKIN PIE (FORMS ITS OWN CRUST)

1/4 c. butter, melted	2 eggs
1/2 c. honey or sorghum	1/2 t. salt
1 1/2 c. pumpkin	1/4 t. ginger
1/2 c. wheat flour	1/4 t. nutmeg
1/2 t. cinnamon	1 1/2 c. milk

Separate eggs. Put yolks in large bowl and add other ingredients beating well. Beat egg whites and fold in last. Pour into pie pan. Bake at 425° for 15 minutes, then at 350° for 45 minutes or until filling is set.

SPICY PUMPKIN PIE (FOR THOSE ALLERGIC TO MILK)

pastry for 9 inch one-crust pie	1/4 c. whole wheat flour
2 c. mashed pumpkin	1/2 t. salt
1/2 c. honey	1/4 t. ginger
1 t. cinnamon	1/4 t. nutmeg
2 eggs	1/8 t. cloves

Separate eggs, put yolks in large bowl and beat. Add rest of ingredients and beat well. Beat egg whites until stiff. Then fold in last. Pour into pie crusts. Bake at 425° for 15 minutes, then at 350° for 45 minutes or until filling is set.

WHOLE WHEAT PASTRY

3 c. whole wheat pastry flour	5 T. cold water
1 c. butter (scant)	1/2 t. salt
1 egg, slightly beaten	1 T. vinegar

In mixing bowl, combine flour, salt, and butter. Blend together until crumbly. Combine egg, water, and vinegar. Stir into flour with fork until ingredients are moistened. With hands, mold into a ball. Chill at least 15 minutes before rolling. Divide pastry in half and press into a ball. Roll out between 2 squares of waxed paper. Remove top sheet of paper and invert pastry over a pie pan, easing it gently into the pan. Remove waxed paper and fit the pastry into the pan without stretching. Roll out second half of pastry. Moisten edge of bottom pastry, along edge of pan, with water or milk. Place second half of pastry over filling. Press top and bottom pastries together along rim. Trim off along edge and flute. Moisten top with the back of a spoon, dipped in milk, to aid browning. Make a few vents in top to allow steam to escape, and bake according to directions. Makes enough pastry for a 2-crust 9 inch pie or 2 single crust pies.

For pie shells: Fit pastry into 2 pans. Flute and prick entire surface with fork. Bake at 450° for 8 - 10 minutes or until lightly browned.

Variation: Use 1/2 c. oil instead of butter. Combine it with the rest of the liquid before adding to the flour.

PIES

When changing a recipe from white flour to whole grain flour, double the spices, or sometimes triple them. Whole grain baked items tend to be more bland and spices are rich in trace elements, so use them generously.

DELICIOUS WHOLE WHEAT PASTRY CRUST

2 c. sifted whole wheat pastry flour

1 t. salt

3/4 c. butter (scant)

4 - 5 T. ice water

2 T. wheat germ

Sift flour and salt. Add wheat germ. With pastry cutter, blend in butter. Sprinkle ice water over mixture and blend with fork. Pastry should be just moist enough to hold together.

CRUST FOR DESSERTS▼

1 stick butter

1 c. flour

1/2 c. nuts if desired

Mix together and bake in loaf pan until brown (approximately 20 minutes). Crumble as soon as you can. This crust can be used instead of graham cracker crust.

ALL-BRAN PIE CRUST▼

1 c. quick-cooking oats

1/4 c. oat bran

1/4 c. wheat bran

1/4 c. walnut pieces

2 egg whites

1 T. melted butter

Combine oats, brans, and nuts. In another bowl, beat egg whites until it peaks. Pour butter into oat mixture and mix well. Then add egg whites. Pour into greased pie pan and press crust onto the bottom and the sides.

Bake until light brown, firm, and dry to the touch (about 15 minutes). Chill. Makes 1 crust.

BARLEY PIE CRUST▾

3/4 c. butter
2 c. barley flour

1 egg
1 T. water

Mix all ingredients. Crust will be crumbly. Roll between waxed paper and fit into pie plate.

Note: This pie crust cannot be baked in advance on its own. It must be baked with a filling in it.

COCONUT PIE SHELL▾

1 1/2 c. unsweetened coconut
2 1/2 T. butter

Mix and pat into pie pan. Bake in 350° oven until edges brown. Cool before filling.

GRANOLA PIE CRUST

2 c. granola
2 t. honey
1/4 c. butter, melted

Combine ingredients well. Press evenly over bottom and sides of 9 inch pie pan. Bake at 350° for 6 - 8 minutes or until lightly browned. Cool and fill with your favorite pie filling.

OATMEAL PIE CRUST

1 c. quick oats
3/4 c. wheat flour
1/3 c. honey

1/4 t. salt
6 T. butter

Mix altogether and press into greased pie plate. Bake at 350° for 15 - 20 minutes.

Use a little cornmeal in pie dough recipes for a more flaky crust.

148

PIES

Instead of rolling out whole wheat pie crusts, press them into the pie plates with floured fingers. This isn't nearly as frustrating as trying to roll them out.

NUT PIE SHELL

1 3/4 c. ground nuts   1 T. butter
1 T. honey
   Mix all ingredients and pat into pie plate. Toast at 350° for 10 minutes or serve raw. Cool shell before filling.

PIE CRUST

1 1/2 c. wheat flour   1/3 c. ice water
1 T. cornmeal   honey
6 T. butter   salt

PIE DOUGH

2 1/2 c. wheat flour   1/2 c. cream, or as needed
1 t. baking powder   1/2 t. salt
1 T. vinegar   1/2 c. butter
1/4 c. water   1 egg
   Makes 4 - 1 crust pies.

RICE PIE CRUST

3/4 c. butter   1 T. water
1 1/2 c. rice flour   1 egg
   Mix all ingredients together well. Roll between waxed paper and fit into pie plate. Bake at 350° for 8 - 10 minutes.
   Note: This pie crust must be baked first without a filling in it.

desserts

Honey is twice as sweet as sugar, so it doesn't take as much. Buy honey which you know has not been processed. Processed, over-heated honey will pour out in a thin stream weeks after you buy it. Raw honey usually gets thick ("sug-ary") soon after you buy it and especially when stored in a cool place.

APPLE CRISP

4 c. sliced apples	1 T. ReaLemon
1/3 c. whole wheat flour	1 c. oatmeal
1/4 c. honey	1/3 c. melted butter
1 t. cinnamon	

Place apples in buttered pan. Sprinkle with lemon and honey. Combine dry ingredients. Add butter. Mix until it crumbles. Pour over apples and bake at 350° for 30 minutes or until tender.

Serve warm with homemade ice cream. Delicious!

APPLE CRUMBLE

2 c. unsweetened shredded coconut
1 c. wheat germ
1/3 c. (scant) honey
1/4 c. oil

Mix coconut and wheat germ. Mix oil and honey. Now mix the 2 together. Using a little over half, press into an oiled pie pan. Put apple mixture (below) into pressed crust, sprinkling remaining crumbs over top of apple mixture.

Filling:

6 medium cooking apples, peeled and sliced

3 T. minute tapioca	3/4 t. nutmeg
2 1/2 t. cinnamon	2 T. butter
2 t. lemon juice	3 T. water
1/3 c. honey	

Combine all the ingredients except the apples. Pour over the apples and mix thoroughly. Pour into crust-lined pan (above). Top with remaining crumbs. Bake at 325° for 30 minutes.

Note: This pie is very tasty but crumbly. Coconut and wheat germ, to our surprise, is a delicious blend. We like the pie and use a spoon to get it out of the pan. (Who says pie has to be in wedges?)

APPLE CRUNCH

Grease a 9 x 13 cake pan with butter. Fill half full with raw grated apples. Sprinkle with cinnamon. Mix in a 1/2 c. of honey. Top with the following crumbs.

1 1/2 c. oatmeal	1/2 t. salt
1 c. wheat flour	1/3 c. butter
1/2 c. peanut butter	

Bake in moderate oven until nicely browned and apples are bubbly and done. Serve warm with cold milk.

FRUIT GOODIE

1 c. pitted dates	1 c. raisins
1 c. water	

Chop or blend fruit. Then add water and boil for 3 minutes. Add 1/2 c. melted butter. Stir and cool.

In a mixing bowl, blend date mixture with:

2 c. whole wheat pastry flour	2 eggs
1 t. baking soda	1 t. vanilla

Mix well and add:

8 oz. unsweetened crushed pineapple

1 c. coconut

1/2 c. grated carrots

1 c. walnut pieces

Pour into greased and floured oblong pan. Bake 25 - 30 minutes at 375°. When cool, it may be topped with frosting of 8 oz. unsweetened crushed pineapple mixed with 6 oz. softened cream cheese.

DESSERTS

"Sugary" honey can be heated until it is clear and will pour again. Place honey in a glass container, uncovered, and set in water in a large stainless steel container and heat SLOWLY over LOW heat. During the summer just set it outside in the sun. Too high heat kills the enzymes.

APPLE GOODIE

1/4 c. honey	2 t. cinnamon
2 T. whole wheat flour	1/4 t. nutmeg
1/2 t. salt	4 1/2 c. sliced apples
Top part:	
1 3/4 c. oatmeal	1/2 t. baking powder
1/2 c. honey	1 1/2 t. vanilla
1 c. wheat flour	1 t. cinnamon
1/2 t. baking soda	6 T. butter

Mix together first 5 ingredients, then mix with apples. Put on bottom of greased pan.

Mix ingredients of top part until crumbly, put on top of apples, and pat firmly. Bake at 350° for 30 minutes or until brown and crust is formed.

SUMMER FRUIT COBBLER

2 qts. cubed apples	2 c. peaches (chopped)
1 qt. blackberries	2/3 c. honey

Stir together. Bake at 425° for 30 minutes.

1 1/2 c. wheat flour	1/8 t. salt
1/4 t. allspice	3/4 t. baking soda
1 1/2 c. oatmeal or wheat flakes	

Stir altogether.

1/3 c. honey	1/4 c. oil

Stir into above until crumbly.

Sprinkle on top of fruit. Bake at 350° for 20 minutes.

Note: You could use any fruit of your choice.

PEACH CRISP

6 c. well-ripened fresh peaches
1/3 c. whole wheat or rye flour
1 c. oatmeal
1/3 c. butter, melted

Preheat oven to 375°. Place peaches in baking dish. Combine dry ingredients. Add butter and mix until crumbly. Sprinkle on top of peaches. Bake for 30 minutes.

BROWN BETTY

3 c. oatmeal
1 c. maple syrup
1 t. salt

1 c. wheat flour
1 c. melted butter

Spread over 2 qts. cut up peaches. Bake at 350° for 45 minutes.

TEN DOLLAR FRUIT PIE

1/2 c. oatmeal
1 c. whole wheat flour
1 1/2 c. honey

1 c. milk
1 t. salt
1 T. baking powder

Make batter of these.

Melt a full 1/2 c. butter in cake pan. Pour batter into this. Heat one qt. canned sour cherries or peaches (other fruit may be used if desired) and pour into batter. Bake at 375° for 30 minutes.

This is delicious if served warm with cold milk.

DESSERTS

DESSERTS

FLUFFY TAPIOCA CREAM

Beat until foamy:

1 egg white

Add:

· 1 T. honey

Beat until it stand in soft peaks. Set aside.

Mix in saucepan:

1 egg yolk	2 c. milk
1 1/2 T. honey	1/8 t. salt
3 T. minute tapioca	

Cook and stir until mixture comes to a full boil. Remove from heat and blend gradually into egg whites. Add 1/2 t. vanilla. Let stand. Stir after 15 - 20 minutes. Let cool.

COOKED APPLES

Cut apples in half (peel if you wish). Place in baking dish or medium saucepan. Mix together 2 1/2 T. whole wheat flour, 1/2 c. honey or maple syrup, and enough water to make a smooth sauce. Dot apples with butter and sprinkle generously with cinnamon. Pour sauce over apples and bake or cook on top of stove using the Lifetime method.

SPICED APPLES

4 c. sliced apples	2 1/2 t. cinnamon
1/2 c. butter	1/3 c. apple juice
1/4 c. honey	1/2 c. yogurt

Cook apples in hot butter. Stir constantly until soft and golden brown. Add honey, cinnamon, and apple juice. Cook 5 minutes more. Remove from heat, cool, and fold in yogurt. These apples may be served warm or cold.

BANANA PINEAPPLE CRISP

2 T. butter	2 T. honey

1 - 20 oz. can crushed unsweetened pineapple with juice

1 t. cinnamon	3 bananas, sliced
1 1/2 T. cold water	1 t. nutmeg
1/2 c. unsweetened shredded coconut	1 T. cornstarch

Crust:

3/4 c. unsweetened shredded coconut	2 1/2 T. honey
	1 1/2 T. oil
1/3 c. wheat germ	

Melt butter in medium-sized saucepan. Stir in honey, pineapple with juice, nutmeg, and cinnamon. Mix cornstarch and water. Stir into pineapple mixture. Bring to a boil and boil for 1 minute, stirring constantly. Slice bananas and arrange in a baking dish. Sprinkle with coconut. Pour the pineapple mixture over the bananas and coconut and top with crust. Bake for 20 minutes at 375°.

To Make Crust: Mix coconut and wheat germ. Blend oil and honey together and mix with coconut mixture. Sprinkle over pineapple mixture and bake as directed above.

CHERRY PUDDING

2 c. sifted whole wheat flour	2 t. baking powder
1/2 t. salt	2 T. melted butter
1/2 - 2/3 c. sorghum or maple syrup	1 c. milk

Sift dry ingredients together. Add sorghum, milk, and butter and mix until blended. Pour into pan and cover with cherry sauce.

2 - 3 c. sour cherries	2 T. melted butter
1 c. hot cherry juice	

Bake at 400° for 40 - 50 minutes or until done. This is delicious eaten warm with milk or ice cream. For an extra special dish, sprinkle top with pecans before baking.

DESSERTS

Regular jello is mostly sugar. The sugar-free kind has additives and preservatives. Use Knox gelatin.

DESSERTS

CAROB CORNSTARCH PUDDING

Heat to boiling:

1 qt. milk	1/2 t. salt
2/3 c. honey	

Make a thickening of:

1/2 c. milk	1/2 c. cornstarch
2 eggs	2 T. carob

When milk begins to bubble, stir in thickening and bring back to a boil. Remove from heat and stir in 1 t. vanilla.

Variation: For Vanilla Pudding, use only 1/2 c. honey and omit carob.

Note: It is important to add the honey to the milk before the cornstarch. If added afterwards, the pudding will turn thin for some reason.

COTTAGE CHEESE PUDDING

2 c. cottage cheese	1/2 t. salt
1/4 c. honey	2 t. cinnamon
2 T. wheat flour	1/2 t. nutmeg
2 beaten eggs	2 c. milk

Blend altogether in blender jar for 3 - 4 minutes. This will make the pudding smooth. Pour into baking dish. Bake at 350° for 1 hour.

DANISH RASPBERRY PUDDING

3 t. lemon juice
3 c. mashed raspberries or strawberries

1/2 c. honey	3 T. butter
2 T. cornstarch	1/2 t. salt
1 3/4 c. milk	1 c. yogurt

Mix lemon juice and raspberries and set in refrigerator to chill. Melt butter and add honey, salt, and milk. Bring to a boil and thicken with cornstarch. Chill. Just before serving, fold together raspberries and yogurt. Add chilled mixture, stirring until smooth. Serves 6 - 8.

DATE PUDDING

Pour 1 c. boiling water over 1 c. cut-up dates. Set aside to cool. Measure and sift into bowl:

1 1/2 c. wheat flour	1 t. baking soda
1 t. baking powder	1/2 t. salt

Add:

1/4 c. sorghum or maple syrup

2 T. melted butter	1 egg
date mixture	1 c. nuts

Mix and pour into large loaf pan. Pour sauce over the top, made up of the following:

1 1/2 c. boiling water	1 T. butter
1/4 c. maple syrup	

Bake at 350° for 30 minutes or until done. Serve with whipped cream.

DESSERTS

When whipping cream, add honey just before you're finished whipping and continue whipping a minute. Try using other flavorings at times instead of vanilla, such as almond extract, maple, peppermint, etc. When using vanilla, try a few sprinkles of nutmeg with it.

DESSERTS

Light colored honey is preferable to use for baking. It does not have the heavy flavors of dark honey.

DATE PUDDING

Cake part:

1 t. baking soda sprinkled on 1 c. chopped dates

Add 1 c. boiling water and let set until cool. Mix ingredients below, then add to date mixture.

1 egg	1/2 c. honey
1 T. butter	pinch of salt
1 1/2 c. whole wheat flour	1 t. baking powder

1/2 c. chopped walnuts, saving a little to garnish top of pudding

Bake at 375° for 25 minutes.

Whip together:

1 pt. cream	honey to taste
1/2 t. vanilla	

It's a little tricky to add honey to whipped cream. Add before cream is quite whipped, then finish as usual.

Cut cake into 1/2 - 3/4 inch squares. Layer into a clear glass bowl: cake, 2 - 3 bananas cut up, and whipped cream. Make sure you put whipped cream on top. Lastly, sprinkle chopped walnuts on top.

RICE PUDDING

2 1/2 c. cooked carrots or pumpkin

1 1/4 c. cooked brown rice	2 1/2 T. olive oil
1/4 c. apple juice	1 beaten egg
1 T. sweetener	1/2 c. raisins

pinch each of nutmeg, cinnamon, and ginger

Bake at 350° for 30 - 40 minutes. (Place the baking dish in a larger pan with 1 inch water when in the oven to prevent scorching.)

This is good to eat cold.

RICE PUDDING

2 c. cooked, cold, brown rice

1/2 c. apple, pear, or peach juice (or milk)

1/2 - 2/3 c. honey or maple syrup

2 eggs, beaten,
    or 2 T. arrowroot powder plus 1 t. guar gum powder

2 t. vanilla	1 - 1 1/2 t. cinnamon
1/8 t. sea salt	1/8 t. nutmeg

1/2 c. raisins or currants (optional)

   Plain, left-over brown rice may be used, or sweet brown rice. 1 c. dry rice usually makes 2 c. cooked. Mix all the ingredients together. Pour them into a lightly oiled 9 x 9 inch casserole dish. Bake for 35 - 45 minutes, uncovered, at 375° until "set" and somewhat firm. Serve hot or cold with milk, cream, or nut or soy milk.

YOGURT RICE PUDDING

2 c. cooked brown rice	2 bananas, sliced and chopped
1 c. plain yogurt	1/4 c. maple syrup (scant)
1 c. drained, crushed pineapple	

   Mix and chill well.

PUMPKIN CUSTARD

6 eggs – separate them and beat yolks
    Add:

4 c. cooked pumpkin	1 t. cinnamon
3 T. whole wheat flour	1 t. nutmeg
6 c. milk	1 c. honey, sorghum, or maple syrup

   Now beat and add egg whites.

DESSERTS

PUMPKIN PUDDING

1 1/2 c. cooked pumpkin	1/2 t. salt
1/4 c. wheat flour	2 t. cinnamon
2 eggs	3/4 t. lemon flavor
2 t. vanilla	2 c. milk
1/2 c. honey	

Blend altogether in blender pitcher for 1 minute. Pour into baking dish. Sprinkle cinnamon on top. Bake at 350° for 60 minutes.

STEAMED GRAHAM PUDDING

1 egg	1 c. maple syrup
1 c. sour milk	2 T. molasses
2 c. whole wheat flour	1 t. baking soda
1/2 t. cinnamon	1/2 t. cloves
1/2 t. salt	1/2 c. raisins

Steam on top of stove, preferably using an angel food cake pan. Set in a large covered kettle. Simmer 1 - 1 1/2 hours. Serve warm with milk. Very good and economically made.

TAPIOCA PUDDING

2 eggs, slightly beaten	3 1/2 c. milk
1/3 c. honey	6 T. minute tapioca
1/4 t. salt	1 1/2 t. vanilla

Mix all ingredients, except vanilla, in saucepan. Let stand 5 minutes. Cook over low medium heat, stirring constantly until mixture comes to a full boil. Cook until tapioca dissolves. Pudding thickens as it cools. Stir once after 20 minutes. Serve warm or cold. It is good with bananas.

STRAWBERRY SHORTCAKE

4 c. whole wheat flour
1 t. salt
1 1/2 c. milk
6 t. baking powder
4 T. maple syrup
1/2 c. butter

Bake at 425° for 20 minutes. Serve with milk and strawberries.

CREAM CHEESE DESSERT

Make cream cheese by draining 1 qt. yogurt in cheese cloth until stiff.

Roll a few graham crackers and add a little melted butter. Press crumbs into bottom of 9 x 13 pan.

Whip 1 cup cream.

Blend 1 cup hot water in blender on high speed, and add 2 T. gelatin and 1/2 cup honey. Then blend in 2 or 3 ice cubes. Pour into a bowl and fold in whipped cream.

In mixer bowl, beat 1 - 2 cups of cream cheese. Add 1/4 cup honey. Add gelatin and cream to this and beat until smooth. Pour over graham cracker crumbs. Chill while thickening strawberries, blueberries, or pineapple for a topping.

Before heating milk in a saucepan, rinse the pan in cold water and it will not scorch so quickly.

NOTES

ice cream and frozen desserts

ICE CREAM AND
FROZEN DESSERTS

Eggs will beat up fluffier if al-
lowed to come to room temperature before beating.

DELICIOUS ICE CREAM

4 c. milk	honey to taste
1 T. vanilla	5 t. plain gelatin

Dissolve gelatin in 1 c. of the milk. Heat the remaining 3 c. of milk but do not boil. Add remaining ingredients and stir to dissolve. Pour into pan and freeze.

When ready to use, let thaw 15 - 20 minutes so you can dig it out with a spoon.

In blender jar, alternately add frozen mixture, milk, vanilla, and honey to taste until you have the right consistency. With practice, you'll catch on. Serve immediately.

Variations: A little carob powder may be used in place of vanilla when blending. This gives it a chocolate flavor.

Try yogurt in place of milk and frozen fruit, peaches, strawberries, or blueberries, in place of half of the frozen mixture. We especially like this.

Note: If made too far in advance, this ice cream will be more like pudding.

ICE CREAM (6 QT. FREEZER)

6 eggs, beaten	pinch of salt
1 - 2 c. maple syrup	1 t. vanilla or maple flavoring
honey or sorghum	
2 qts. cream (more or less), then fill up with milk	

Separate eggs and beat. In another bowl beat cream and add maple syrup, vanilla, and salt. Fold in egg yolks then add egg whites last. Pour into freezer and fill up with milk up to 2" from top of can. Freeze.

NUTRITIOUS ICE CREAM

2 c. soy milk	1 c. almonds
1/2 c. sunflower seeds	1/2 c. honey
1/3 c. sesame seeds	1/4 c. oil

Combine all ingredients thoroughly in a blender. While blender is running, drop in 4 c. frozen strawberries. Blend until all berries are thoroughly ground. Carefully stir down any berries on top. Serve immediately or keep in freezer, stirring occasionally.

DAIRY QUEEN ICE CREAM (FOR 5 QT. FREEZER)

Soften 2 T. gelatin in 1/2 c. water. Heat 2 c. milk. Stir softened gelatin into hot milk. Add:

1/2 t. salt	1 1/2 c. honey

Pour mixture into freezer can. Add 2 or 3 c. cream, 5 beaten eggs, and then enough milk to fill can to FILL line. Add 1 T. vanilla.

BANANA ICE CREAM

8 eggs	2 T. vanilla
1 1/4 c. honey	1/2 t. salt
1 pt. cream	1 or 2 mashed bananas*

milk as needed to fill can to within 3 - 4 inches from the top

*1 c. of any kind of fresh fruit may be used instead of bananas.

This is for a 1 1/2 gallon freezer.

ICE MILK

Take the above recipe and omit the cream and freeze. You'll hardly notice the difference.

ICE CREAM AND
FROZEN DESSERTS

HONEY ICE CREAM

1 pt. cream	1/4 t. salt
1 1/4 c. honey	3 eggs
1/2 box plain gelatin	3 t. vanilla
3 pts. + 1 c. milk	

Put gelatin in 1 c. of cold milk and let stand 5 minutes. Heat, but do not boil, 1 pt. of the milk. Stir into hot milk well beaten egg yolks and soaked gelatin. Pour through wire strainer. Stir honey into balance of cold milk and add to gelatin mixture. Whip cream if possible. It is not necessary, but it makes smoother cream. Add salt and vanilla. Last, add stiffly beaten egg whites. Freeze.

Note: This ice cream can be served at once but it is better if you let it stand a few hours. Makes 1 gallon.

PEACH ICE CREAM

3 c. fresh or canned sliced peaches

1/3 c. honey	2 c. yogurt
1/3 - 1/2 c. peach juice	1 t. vanilla

If peaches are fresh, pour honey over them and let them set a bit so they will make juice. Add all the ingredients, except peaches, and beat until smooth. Fold in peaches. Put in freezer container and freeze. Stir once or twice while freezing.

ALMOND ICE CREAM

1 1/2 T. unflavored gelatin	1 1/2 c. yogurt
1 1/4 c. pineapple juice	1 t. almond extract
1 c. orange juice	1/4 t. salt
4 T. lemon juice	3/4 c. ground almonds
1 1/4 c. honey	1 c. heavy cream, whipped

Sprinkle gelatin on pineapple juice in saucepan. Add honey and heat, stirring until gelatin is dissolved. Cool. Add orange and lemon juice. Blend yogurt with almond extract, salt, and almonds. Stir in first mixture and fold in whipped cream. Pour into freezer container and freeze until firm, stirring a couple of times. Serves 6 - 8.

ICE CREAM AND
FROZEN DESSERTS

BLUEBERRY SMOOTHIE▾

1 c. blueberries
2 peaches, seeds removed (optional)
1 frozen banana
1 c. orange or apple juice

Whirl all ingredients in blender until smooth.

Note: Smoothies are combination fruit drinks that are made in a blender. Since they include the pulp, they are thicker than regular fruit juices and are therefore more filling. Children of all ages love smoothies.

APPLE DATE SMOOTHIE▾

2 bananas, fresh or frozen	2 - 4 large dates, seeds removed
2 apples, peeled and cored	1 c. fresh apple juice

Whirl all ingredients in blender until smooth.

**ICE CREAM AND
FROZEN DESSERT**

APRICOT-PEACH SMOOTHIE▾

2 peaches, seeds removed, peeled if desired

4 apricots, seeds removed

2 bananas, fresh or frozen

1 c. fresh orange or apple juice

   Whirl all ingredients in blender until smooth.

FROZEN STRAWBERRY DESSERT

   Beat 8 oz. softened cream cheese with 1/3 c. honey.

   In another bowl, put:

1 large can crushed pineapple (drained)

1 1/2 c. frozen strawberries   2 bananas, sliced

1/2 c. chopped nuts   1 large bowl whipped cream

   Mix thoroughly but gently. Combine with cream cheese mixture. Spoon into loaf pan and freeze overnight.

   Serve frozen. Cut into slices. This keeps 4 - 6 weeks in freezer. Yields 12 - 14 servings.

FROZEN FRUIT

   Mix 1 1/2 c. maple syrup with 3 c. hot water.

   Add:

6 oz. lemonade   6 oz. orange juice

2 c. fruit cocktail   1 can crushed pineapple.

   Slice in 6 - 8 bananas and freeze.

PINEAPPLE SHAKE

1 - 20 oz. can pineapple, chunks or crushed

1 c. yogurt   honey to taste if desired

6 milk ice cubes   1 banana

   Put all ingredients, except ice, in blender and whir. Add ice slowly, blending thoroughly. Serve.

ORANGE SLUSH

3 c. water   6 bananas (sliced or crushed)

1 can crushed pineapple   1 c. maple syrup

1 can frozen orange juice
   Freeze and eat.

ORANGE SHERBET

2 1/2 c. orange juice   pinch of salt

2 1/2 t. unflavored gelatin   1 1/2 c. yogurt

1/3 c. honey

   Soften gelatin in 1/2 c. of the orange juice and heat until dissolved. Add honey and salt. Cool by adding remaining orange juice. Pour into a freezer container and freeze to a soft mush. Add yogurt and beat until smooth. Return to freezer and freeze until firm.

ICE CREAM AND
FROZEN DESSERTS

ICE CREAM AND
FROZEN DESSERTS

HOT BLUEBERRY SAUCE

1/2 c. water

2 T. maple syrup or honey

1 t. lemon juice

1 T. arrowroot flour

2 c. blueberries

Combine water and arrowroot in saucepan. Stir over low heat until thick. Stir in blueberries, maple syrup, and lemon juice . . . Experiment with other berries and adding chopped nuts. Serve over pancakes, yogurt, or ice cream.

ICE CREAM SANDWICHES

Take 2 Whoopie Pies (recipe in Cookie section) and fill with frozen yogurt. Place back in freezer until frozen hard.

BANANA SPLIT

Cut bananas in half, lengthwise. Use 2 halves for one serving. Put yogurt or cottage cheese on each serving. Top with honey or sugarless jam and any sliced or chopped fresh fruit. Sprinkle with wheat germ or chopped nuts.

Variation: Try frozen yogurt and an ice cream syrup.

wholesome
snacks

CREAM CHEESE BALLS

1 lb. cream cheese

3/4 c. chopped dates

1 T. lemon or orange juice

3/4 c. almond, sesame, or sunflower seeds

1/2 c. unsweetened coconut

1/2 t. allspice

Soften cream cheese. Mix dates with small amount of flour to separate. Mix well all dry ingredients except nuts. Blend in cream cheese. Squeeze everything together in your hands. Shape into 1 inch balls. Roll in nuts.

CHEESE BALL

1 lb. cream cheese

1 lb. Colby cheese

1 T. dried onion flakes

1 t. garlic salt

1 t. Worcestershire sauce

Mix at room temperature and form into ball. Roll in mixture of walnut pieces and parsley flakes. Chill.

PEANUT BUTTER BALLS▾

1/3 c. peanut butter

1/4 c. chopped nuts

2/3 c. unsweetened coconut

1 t. lemon juice

1 t. vanilla

1/2 c. raisins

Mix altogether and form into bite-sized balls. Chill until firm.

ALMOND OR PEANUT BUTTER BALLS

1 c. almond butter or peanut butter
1/2 c. maple syrup or honey   1/2 c. sesame seeds
1 c. fine coconut

Mix well. Form into balls and roll in fine coconut or ground nuts. Refrigerate. These will keep a long time.

POPCORN CRUNCH

1/2 c. melted butter   1/2 c. honey
3 qts. popped popcorn

Heat butter and honey until blended. Pour over popcorn and mix well. Spread on cookie sheet in thin layer. Bake in preheated 350° oven for 10 minutes until crisp.

PEANUT BUTTER FUDGE

3/4 c. milk powder   1/2 c. honey
3/4 c. peanut butter   1 t. vanilla

Mix peanut butter, honey, and vanilla. Blend in milk powder, using hands when mixture becomes stiff. Pat into 8" square baking pan. Chill. Cut into squares.

Variation: Roll fudge into balls and roll in sesame seeds.

WHOLESOME SNACKS

Popcorn will stay fresh and you will eliminate "old maids" if you store it in the freezer.

CAROB OATMEAL CANDY

3/4 c. honey	3 c. quick oats
1/4 c. butter	1/2 c. shredded coconut
1/4 c. carob powder	1 t. vanilla
1/4 c. milk	1/2 c. peanut butter

Combine first 4 ingredients into sauce pan. Boil rapidly for 2 minutes. Remove from heat and add the remaining ingredients. Spoon onto waxed paper.

OATMEAL CANDY COOKIES

1 c. honey	3 3/4 c. oatmeal
1/2 c. milk	1/2 c. carob powder
1/4 c. butter	1 c. shredded coconut
1 c. ground nuts	

Combine honey, milk, and butter in a saucepan. Boil 1 minutes, stirring constantly. Mix dry ingredient all together. Pour boiled mixture over dry ingredients. Stir well and form into balls. Cool. Store in a tight container.

Variation: Add 2 t. vanilla and 1/4 c. peanut butter to boiled mixture before mixing with dry ingredients.

DANDY CANDY▾

1 1/4 c. peanut butter	1 1/4 c. milk powder

Combine all ingredients with a fork or spoon until well blended. Shape into balls or roll into logs. Roll in coconut, wheat germ, or sesame seeds, or a combination of all three. Put on cookie sheet or platter or pat into pan. Set, covered, in refrigerator for 1 hour to chill, or in freezer 15 - 20 minutes. Slice into bite size pieces.

Variation: For fudge candy, add 1/3 c. carob powder. For chewy candy, add 3/4 c. rolled oats. For crunchy candy, add 3/4 c. puffed cereal.

CHEWY CHARLIES

1 c. peanut butter	1 c. dry milk
1 c. raisins	1/2 c. honey

Mix all ingredients. May be rolled in Rice Krispies or coconut, or they can be left plain.

DATE BALLS

Boil together:

1 lb. dates	1/4 c. honey
1/2 c. water	lemon flavoring

Fold in all the Crispy Brown Rice Cereal it will hold. Shape into balls and roll in sesame seeds or coconut, or put in pan lined with graham crackers.

PEANUT BUTTER POPCORN

4 qts. popped corn	1 1/2 c. peanut butter
1 1/2 c. honey	1 1/2 t. vanilla
1/2 c. baking molasses	

Keep corn warm in a 250° oven. Mix honey and molasses, bring to a boil for half a minute. Remove from heat and beat in peanut butter and vanilla. Pour syrup over popcorn and mix well. Mold into balls, working rapidly. Makes 16 balls.

WHOLESOME SNACKS

Cheese won't harden if you butter the exposed edges before storing.

PLAYGROUND SNACK MIX

1 c. sunflower seeds   1/3 c. cashew pieces

1/3 c. raw almonds   1/3 c. dried apples

1/3 c. ribbon coconut, unsweetened

1 c. raisins or currants

    Combine all ingredients. Wrap in 6 individual serving bags.

    Note: 1/2 c. carob chips may be added for an extra treat.

CHILDREN'S GARDEN MIX

1 c. hulled pumpkin seeds   1 c. pecans or walnuts, raw

1/2 c. filberts or brazil nuts   1/2 c. dried apricots

1/2 c. dried pears or peaches

    Combine all ingredients. Wrap in 6 individual serving bags.

    Note: 1/2 c. carob chips may be added for an extra treat.

CHEESE STICKS

1 3/4 c. flour   3/4 c. grated strong cheese

1/2 c. butter   1 t. salt

6 - 7 T. cold water   1/2 t. paprika

    Measure flour, add salt, and cut in butter. Add water, form into a ball, and chill. Roll out 1/4 inch thick. Cut into 1/2 inch strips, 5 inches long. Twist. Bake on ungreased cookie sheet at 450° for 10 - 12 minutes.

BREADSTICKS FOR TODDLERS

1 1/4 c. wheat flour
2 t. cinnamon
1 t. baking soda
1 c. grated cheese
1/3 c. butter
1/4 t. salt
3 T. milk
1 egg, beaten

Mix together dry ingredients, except cheese. Cut in cheese and butter until mixture resembles coarse crumbs. Blend milk with beaten egg and add to crumbs. Stir with fork or hands until dough clings together.

Taking teaspoonfuls of dough, roll into little sticks. Arrange 1 inch apart on greased cookie sheets. Salt may be sprinkled on the sticks if desired. Bake for 15 minutes at 350°.

TEETHING BISCUITS, CRACKERS, OR BREADSTICKS

When making bread, save out a little dough after the first time it rises. For teething biscuits or crackers:

Knead in a little more wheat flour. On floured board, roll out dough to 1/8 inch thick. Cut into whatever shape you desire: squares, rectangles, or sticks. Arrange close together but not touching on a greased cookie sheet. Prick with a fork and sprinkle with a little salt if desired. Bake until lightly browned at 325°. Cool, then store in airtight container.

For breadsticks:
Roll dough into 4 inch long ropes and continue with directions as above.

WHOLESOME SNACKS

WHOLESOME SNACKS

"WHITE" CRACKERS

2 1/2 c. whole wheat pastry flour

1 1/2 t. salt — 1/3 c. butter

3/4 t. baking soda — 2 small eggs

1/2 c. buttermilk OR 1/2 c. milk + 2 T. vinegar

salt for topping if desired

Combine flour, salt, and baking soda. Cut in butter, then add milk and eggs. Blend to make a stiff dough. More flour may be needed, as whole wheat varies a lot. Knead thoroughly.

Roll out 1/8 inch thick, with rolling pin, on floured surface. Cut into squares and place on lightly greased cookie sheets. Prick with fork and sprinkle with salt. Bake at 325° until lightly browned. Watch closely so they don't burn.

GRAHAM CRACKERS

1/2 c. oil — 3 1/2 c. wheat flour

1/2 c. honey — 1 1/2 t. baking powder

1 T. molasses — 1 t. baking soda

2 t. vanilla — 2 t. cinnamon

1/2 t. salt — 1/3 c. milk

Mix oil, honey, molasses, and vanilla in a large bowl. Combine dry ingredients. Add dry mixture to liquids, alternating with milk. Mix well, using hands. If dough is too sticky, add up to 1/2 c. more flour.

Divide dough into quarters. Roll out to 1/4 inch thick with rolling pin. Use table knife to cut dough into squares. Place on cookie sheets and prick with fork. Bake at 300° until outer edges are slightly browned. Let cool a little on cookie sheets before removing crackers. Store in airtight container.

SOFT WHOLE WHEAT PRETZELS

4 t. dry yeast	4 T. oil
1 3/4 c. warm water	2/3 c. non-instant milk powder
2 T. honey	5 c. wheat flour
2 t. salt	3/4 c. wheat germ

Dissolve yeast in water with honey and let set to sponge. Stir in salt, oil, milk powder, and 2 1/2 c. of the flour. Beat until smooth. Add remaining flour and wheat germ to make a soft dough. Knead until smooth and elastic.

Let rise until double. Punch down. Taking balls of dough about the size of 2 walnuts, roll into a rope 16 inches long. The children love to help with this and have lots of ideas for shapes. You could make letters and numbers besides the traditional pretzel shape.

Place pretzels onto greased cookie sheets and let rise 20 minutes. Or, if in a hurry, they may be popped in the oven right away. Glaze may be made with 1 T. water beaten with 1 egg and brushed on top. Also, you may sprinkle with the topping of your choice: salt, sesame seeds, or poppy seeds. Bake at 350° for 15 minutes or until golden brown. Cool.

If you don't have time to bake them, make the dough into shapes and freeze them. When ready to bake, dip frozen dough in water, sprinkle with salt, and bake for 25 - 30 minutes. The baked pretzels may be frozen. Thaw them 5 - 6 minutes at 350°.

WHOLESOME SNACKS

Running ice cold water over popcorn kernels before popping will eliminate "old maids."

WHOLESOME SNACKS

For "special" ice cubes, put pieces of fruit such as cherries, pineapple chunks, or grapes, etc., in each section of the ice cube trays. Then fill them with water and freeze. The pretty ice cubes also offer a fruit treat after the ice melts.

FRUIT LEATHER▼

A different and tasty treat.

Fruit leather is delicious and chewy. It is ideal for strawberries, peaches, bananas, apricots, and apples, etc. It's nutritious and fun to make.

Select the fruit or any combination of fruits (fresh, frozen, or canned). Drain off excess juice. Wash and pit fresh fruit. Peel if desired. Pureé in a blender or food processor to consistency of thick applesauce. Add a little honey or maple syrup to sweeten, if desired. (Optional: 1 t. lemon juice per two cups of pureéd fruit may be added to preserve color and provide tartness.)

Cover dehydrator screen with plastic wrap. Grease plastic with oil so leather won't stick.

Spread the fruit pureé in a layer 1/8 - 1/4 inch thick on plastic wrap. Position screens in dehydrator. Dry 9 - 16 hours or until moisture is gone. When set and almost dry, turn leather over to finish drying. When no longer sticky and completely dry, remove from plastic wrap. While still warm, it may be rolled into a jelly roll fashion or cut into strips. Wrap in plastic to store.

Caution: Plastic wrap is not able to withstand high temperatures. Use dehydrating temperatures only.

yogurt

YOGURT

Do not overheat yogurt. Whenever possible, add yogurt just before it is completely done.

Fold yogurt in carefully (rather than stirring) to keep its thick consistency.

CAROL'S YOGURT▾

1 gal. whole milk   1/4 c. cold water
8 qt. kettle with domed lid   3/4 c. plain yogurt
4 t. plain gelatin

Heat milk to boiling in kettle. Dissolve gelatin in cold water, pour into boiled milk, and stir. Let milk cool down to 110°. Add plain yogurt and stir thoroughly. Pour into 4 wide mouth quart jars. Fill 8 qt. kettle 1/3 full with warm water (around 100°). Set filled jars in kettle and cover with lid. Set kettle in a warm place (over a pilot light is excellent) for 4 - 6 hours. Yogurt should be like pudding. Drain off water in top of each jar so it doesn't make a scum. Set jars in the refrigerator and let the yogurt get cold before using.

Note: Be sure to save 3/4 c. for culture for next time.

YOGURT▾

Heat 3 qts. milk to almost boiling. Cool slowly to lukewarm, then beat in 1 1/2 c. non-instant dry milk and 1 c. yogurt from your last batch. Pour into jars and put jars in a pan of warm water in a warm place for 4 - 5 hours. Then refrigerate.

"Warm place" could be above the pilot or in an unlit gas oven.

YOGURT WITH FRUIT▾

For yogurt with fruit, add fruit when you are ready to eat it. Don't disturb the culture by stirring when the yogurt is being made.

HOMEMADE YOGURT▾

1 qt. milk   2 T. yogurt
1 c. dry milk

   Heat milk to 175°- 180°. Remove from heat. Cover and let cool to 150°, then add dry milk. Pour into a wide mouth quart jar and let it cool down to 130°. Add 2 heaping T. plain yogurt. Set jar in a kettle of warm water with a lid covering it for 6 - 8 hours or overnight. Put kettle in a warm place like over a pilot light. Refrigerate after it is done and it should be firm.

FROZEN YOGURT

2 t. unflavored gelatin   2 T. honey
2 T. cold water   2 c. plain yogurt
1 T. lemon juice (optional)
1/2 c. fresh fruit (pureéd – frozen or canned)
   Soften gelatin in cold water and lemon juice in a small saucepan for about 1 minute.
   Heat slowly until gelatin is completely dissolved. Cool to room temperature. Whisk gelatin mixture into fruit pureé. Then add honey and yogurt. Mix well. Freeze like you would in making ice cream.

YOGURT WITH FROZEN FRUIT

   Frozen fruit mixed with yogurt when slightly thawed makes it kind of like frozen yogurt. Mix just before serving.

YOGURT

Yogurt may be used in place of buttermilk in many recipes. Add a little water until it is as thin as buttermilk. Yogurt may also be used in place of sour cream and has many less calories.

Stored in refrigerator (at about 40°), yogurt will keep for at least two weeks. It becomes sharper with age.

YOGURT

Mix yogurt with homemade cottage cheese and spread on top of apple buttered bread.

To make yogurt, milk should be heated to 180° to destroy the enzymes that would inhibit fermentation.

CARAMEL YOGURT

Add blackstrap molasses to milk before heating when making yogurt.

YOGURT CREAM CHEESE▼

Put yogurt in a bag made of three layers of cheese cloth. Hang the bag on the kitchen faucet and let drain overnight or until yogurt is the consistency of cream cheese. For a sharper cheese, use yogurt that is several days old. Salt if desired. Use drained yogurt in recipes for dips, spreads, sauces, and dressing when a thicker consistency is desired. 1 quart of yogurt makes 8 oz. of cream cheese.

food
preservation

Carrots, beets, etc. may be buried in a hole for winter storage, unless you're leaving them in the row where they are planted. Cover them well with soil and mulch. Carrots, beets, parsnips, and cabbage stumps (or cores from the heads) may be replanted in the spring, to produce your own seed. Members of the cabbage family; kale, broccoli, cauliflower, etc., will cross-pollinate.

BEAN SOUP (FOR LARGE BATCH TO CAN)

14 pts. or 7 qts. cooked beans	1 1/2 c. catsup
4 c. diced celery	salt and pepper to taste
1 little onion	14 pts. or 7 qts. water
7 pts. hamburger (browned)	4 c. diced carrots

Cook 20 minutes in open kettle, then cold pack 3 hours. Add a pint of milk to a quart of soup to serve.

MINESTRONE

1 onion	1/2 t. rosemary
1 1/2 c. celery	dash of garlic
1/2 c. parsley	2 c. each of broccoli, corn, zucchini,
1/2 c. green peppers	Potatoes, green beans, cabbage,
1/2 c. mushrooms	and peas
4 c. tomato juice	1 c. each of lima, kidney, and navy
1 c. barley	beans (cooked)
1 t. oregano	salt and pepper to taste
2 t. basil	1 - 2 bay leaves

Grind coarse: onion, celery, parsley, peppers, broccoli, carrots, zucchini, potatoes, and cabbage. Cook barley 5 minutes. Mix. Cold pack 3 hours.

VEGETABLE SOUP

12 lbs. hamburger	1 gal. cut-up celery
1 gal. cut-up carrots	3 qts. peas
10 onions	1# brown rice (soaked overnight)
1 qt. navy beans (soaked overnight)	
8 qts. potatoes (cook with peelings, then peel and dice	

Steam each vegetable separately. Add tomato juice to amount you desire (approximately 10 qts.) Season to taste and process 2 hours.

DRESSING MIX▼

5 parts potatoes
4 parts carrots

2 parts celery
1/2 - 1 part onions

   Add salt and water and cold pack. Very handy to open to make dressing
and to use in casseroles.

KETCHUP

4 qts. tomato chunks
1 onion
1 t. pickling spice
1 c. vinegar
4 T. cornstarch

2 T. honey
1 1/4 t. cinnamon
1 t. red pepper
1 t. dry mustard
2 T. salt

   Boil tomatoes, onion, and pickling spice until tender. Put through
Victorio strainer. Dissolve cornstarch in a little of the vinegar and set aside.
Dissolve the rest of the ingredients in the rest of the vinegar. Add to juice.
Boil 1 hour or longer. Add cornstarch and boil another 10 minutes. Put in
jars and seal.

PIZZA SAUCE▼

1 gal. tomato juice
2 green peppers

1 onion, finely cut
1 small hot pepper

   Cook together until thick, 1 hour or more. Then add:

1 t. oregano
1 t. garlic salt
1/2 t. Tabasco sauce or red pepper
3 T. cornstarch

1 t. black pepper
1 T. salt

   Put in jars and cold pack for 30 minutes.

FOOD PRESERVATION

Parsnips need no last minute storing. In a mild winter, they can be
left in the garden, as freezing tends
to improve flavor. If the winter is
severe, they can be buried in a
deep pit in the garden, or pulled
late, and laid side by side in rows,
and covered with 6 - 8 inches of
straw or leaves.

FOOD PRESERVATION

To store carrots, use an old washing machine tub and add some sand.

GREEN TOMATO MINCEMEAT

5 lbs. green tomatoes (14 - 15 c.)
  Grind and drain 2 hours.

5 lbs. apples, chopped	1 T. salt
2 c. honey	1 T. cloves
1 can crushed pineapple	1 T. nutmeg
3 T. lemon juice	1 c. oil
2 c. molasses	1 pt. water
6 c. raisins	1 t. cinnamon
1 c. vinegar	

Make syrup of water, honey, and spices. Add tomatoes and cook 1/2 hour. Then add the rest of the ingredients and cook 45 minutes. Seal in 7 qt. jars.

CHEEZ WHIZ TO CAN

32 lbs. grated Colby cheese	1 qt. milk
3 1/2 c. cream	1/4 lb. butter

Melt together over low heat. Fill pint jars and cold pack 20 minutes. Makes 20 pints.

CANNING STRAWBERRIES WITH TAPIOCA

Place in a heavy boiler in this order:

1/2 c. water	3 qts. strawberries
1/2 c. honey	1/2 c. tapioca

Sprinkle tapioca over the top. Do not stir, so the tapioca will not stick to the bottom. Keep lid on. Turn heat on medium-high until it starts to boil, then turn to simmer. Allow to simmer for 8 minutes. Then can in hot jars. This should fill 2 qt. jars. A little more water may be needed to start with to be sure you don't run short when filling the jars.

HOT PEPPER SAUCE

15 green sweet peppers	2 T. salt
20 - 30 hot peppers	2 T. oregano
2 lbs. onions	1 clove garlic or more
1 peck ripe tomatoes	

Cook peeled tomatoes. Pour off juice using pulp. You may strain, but don't need to. Grind peppers, onion, and garlic. Mix everything together, cook awhile, then can. Process 20 - 30 minutes under 10 lbs. pressure.

Note: This recipe can be changed according to your taste or what's available in the garden. Carrots or finely shredded cabbage can be used, and more or less hot peppers can be used.

This sauce is good on meats or used as sandwich spread. It can even be added to soup or casseroles.

PICKLE RELISH

In evening, grind:

large dishpan of cucumbers	4 onions
8 peppers, red or green	1/2 c. sea salt

Mix well and let set overnight. Drain for a couple of hours.
Add:

1/4 c. honey	2 t. celery seed
1 qt. vinegar	1 t. mustard

Cook just until cucumbers are clear but not mushy. Hot pack in jars.
Note: Children like this relish on bologna sandwiches.

FOOD PRESERVATION

Freezing corn: After husking the ears, blanch it before removing silk. Place 20 - 25 ears of corn in a 20 qt. canner of boiling water for 3 minutes. Remove quickly and place in the sink with cold water. Drain and add cold water several times until well cooled. By this time there is very little silk left on the ears. The few remaining strands can be picked off with fingers as corn is lifted from the last water.

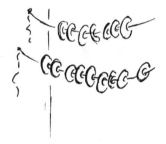

CUCUMBER CARROT RELISH

2 - 3 c. shredded unpeeled cucumbers

1 c. shredded carrots	1 t. celery seed
1/2 c. onion, cut fine	1 t. mustard seed
1 c. honey	1/4 t. turmeric
3/4 c. cider vinegar	

Combine vegetables in a bowl; cover with a plastic bag of ice and let stand 2 hours. Drain well. Combine the remaining ingredients and bring to a boil. Add vegetables and simmer 10 minutes. Pack at once in hot, sterilized jars and seal, or refrigerate mixture to serve fresh. Yield: 2 pints (multiply for large amounts).

SALT AND SUGAR-FREE PICKLES (MAKES 7 PTS.)

Bring to a boil:

4 1/2 c. white vinegar	14 cloves of garlic
4 1/2 c. water	

Sterilize 7 pt. jars. Place in bottom of each jar:

1 grape leaf	3 whole pepper corns
1 strip horseradish 1/2 inch x 3 inch	
1 t. mustard seed	1 whole clove

Fill each jar lightly with cucumber strips. Add 2 sprigs of dill on top of each jar. Pour on vinegar solution to within 1/4 inch of top. Put 2 cloves of garlic in each jar. Tighten lids and process in boiling water for 15 minutes.

PICKLED BEETS

6 c. water (in which beets have been cooked, then strain)

2 c. vinegar	1 t. celery seed
4 c. sorghum	dash of cayenne and cinnamon

Scrub beets with brush, leaving tails and 1 inch of top on. Cook until tender, but do not overcook, using a small amount of water. Put beets in cold water and peel off skins. Cut into desired size pieces. Pack into jars and cover with brine made of the above ingredients. Brine may be adjusted to suit your taste. Add 1 t. salt per quart. Process in hot water bath for 10 minuates.

Note: The brine recipe is supposed to be enough for 10 qts.

TO CAN RED BEETS

3 qts. beets	3 c. vinegar
2 c. maple syrup	(Dilute with water if too strong.
1 1/2 c. water	I take half and half.)
3 T. Indo*	

*Indo is a salt substitute you can buy at the health food stores.

BERRY JAM

8 c. raspberries	1/4 c. apple juice
4 T. lemon juice	4 T. lemon juice
1 1/4 c. honey	

Thoroughly mash raspberries. Add apple juice and lemon juice. Stir together and bring to a boil. Add honey and continue stirring. Boil until mixture has the consistency of thick syrup, being careful not to let it burn. Pour into jars, leaving 1/4 inch headspace. Process in boiling water bath 10 minutes.

Variation: Other berries may be used – strawberries, blueberries, etc. Fruit may be fresh or frozen.

A dampened paper towel or terry cloth brushed downward on a cob of corn will remove every strand of corn silk.

If fresh vegetables are wilted or blemished, pick off the brown edges, sprinkle with cool water, wrap in paper towel and refrigerate for an hour or so.

FRUIT JELLY▾

2 T. lemon juice	dash of salt
2 T. unflavored gelatin	1 pint fruit juice of your choice
2 t. cornstarch	

Combine all ingredients and boil for 2 minutes, stirring constantly. Add sweetener to taste. Makes 1 pint.

APPLE JELLY

3 1/2 lbs. apples   honey

Wash and cut up apples. Remove stems and dark spots, but do not peel or core. Cover apples halfway with water and cook until apple are soft. Drain in a cloth bag. Don't squeeze bag if you want a clear juice. Measure juice and add 1/2 c. honey to each cup of apple juice. Boil until it has the consistency you desire and pour into jars. Process for 5 minutes.

APPLE BUTTER

Combine in large oven kettle:

1 gal. apple juice	2 c. vinegar
2 gal. applesauce	2 T. cinnamon

Boil in oven at 325° - 350° overnight or until as thick as desired. Or you can boil down the apple juice to 1/3 the amount on top of stove first. Then it doesn't take so long in the oven. Honey is optional.

APPLE BUTTER▾

1 gal. apple cider (unsweetened)
1 1/2 qts. applesauce (unsweetened)
Bring to a boil, then turn heat down to let it boil more slowly. Cook about half a day, until desired consistency. Makes about 3 pints.
Note: We make this in the wintertime with canned cider and canned applesauce.

HONEY VINEGAR

Mix together in a crock: 1 quart honey and 8 quarts warm water. Allow to stand in a warm place until fermentation ceases. Makes white vinegar of good quality. Put in jars and seal.

COLE SLAW TO CAN

1 large head cabbage, shredded

3/4 c. shredded carrots	1/2 c. vinegar
2 t. salt	1/2 c. chopped onion
3/4 c. honey	1/2 t. celery seed
1/2 c. chopped celery	1/2 t. mustard seed

Mix together, then put into jars. Process in hot water bath for 10 minutes. This is a real winter treat.

FOOD PRESERVATION

Use Grimes Golden or Summer Rambo apples, nice and ripe, to make a good unsweetened applesauce. Peaches may be canned in slightly weakened unsweetened pineapple juice.

FOOD PRESERVATION

Lettuce and celery keep longer if you store them in paper bags instead of cellophane.

HOMEMADE SAUERKRAUT

Takes 7 - 8, 8 - 10 lbs., heads of cabbage.

Remove damaged outer leaves of cabbage. Wash and cut heads in wedges. Remove core and weigh.

1. Put through kraut cutter (cutter for cole slaw). After shredding 2 or 3 heads, put into 5 gal. crock.

2. Add 3 1/2 T. salt for each 5 lbs. of cabbage. Keep adding more cabbage and salt.

3. When crock is 2/3 full, punch the cabbage down with your fist as hard as you can. Punch down until juice from the cabbage covers the shreds. Crock will be only about 1/3 full. Continue adding shredded cabbage and salt, punching down every so often, until crock is nearly full or you run out of cabbage. Be sure the cabbage juice barely covers the cabbage. Mother Nature does the rest.

4. Lay a dinner plate over the cabbage, weighted down with a jar of water. Cover the whole crock with a tea towel and let the fermentation begin. Keep the crock where the temperature is a steady 65 - 70°. The basement is a good place, where the "working kraut" smell won't offend anyone. Check every other day for a week, skimming off any excess liquid or scum. Make sure liquid still covers the kraut.

5. Every three or four days, stir it up with your hands. Let it continue to ferment for 10 days, then taste it. If you like it, process into canning jars or freezer bags. If you think it is too mild, leave it in the crock a few more days. From this point, however, be sure to check it every day, as spoilage can begin very quickly toward the end of fermentation.

To can kraut, pack it into jars firmly to within a half inch of the top. Follow regular canning procedure, processing 15 minutes in boiling water bath to insure a good seal. The kraut is ready to eat as it comes ot of the jar. We also like several meals right from the crock.

It is very important to use a crock, and not another container.

CANNED PEARS

I had some Keiffer Pears which were not of the best quality, so I cored and peeled them and put them through the food grinder. To 4 qts. ground pears I added 1 can crushed pineapple.

Bring to a boil (a boil that keeps on boiling when stirred). Chill and eat, or put in jars while still boiling, and seal. If you desire more liquid, pineapple juice can be used.

CANNED HAMBURGER

Hamburger may be canned in a pressure canner or the oven. Make sure you purchase only chemical-free meat.

For the pressure canner method: Fill quart jars up to the neck with raw hamburger. If hamburger was frozen, make sure it is completely thawed. Add 1 t. salt to each jar, if desired. Put on lids and tightly screw on rings. Process for 90 minutes at 10 lbs. pressure.

For oven method: Make sure your hamburger is completely thawed, if it was frozen. Fill quart jars up to the neck with raw hamburger. Add 1 t. salt per jar, if desired. Put on lids and screw down lids tightly. Place jars in oven, making sure the jars do not touch each other. Turn oven to 225°. When oven temperature has reached 225°, begin timing after 3 hours. Let jars cool down before removing from oven.

FOOD PRESERVATION

FOOD PRESERVATION

FRUIT VALUE	PROCESS
100%	Raw
95%	Dried
75%	Frozen
50%	Canned
5%	Microwave

When harvesting small amounts of tomatoes, cut them up so they are ready to cook, then freeze. When ready to make ketchup or pizza sauce, thaw overnight. Drain juice off and cook pulp.

Add a little salt to a large container of applesauce while canning, and it will take less sweetener.

FREEZING PEAS

For a real time saver when freezing peas . . . Do not shell peas, just place them in an old pillowcase and place in a large container of boiling water for 3 minutes. Lift out and dump into cold water. Drain and add cold water several times until well cooled. Now shell them. It goes much faster.

STORING CABBAGE

The best results we've experienced in storing cabbage over winter is by digging a trench in the garden. Line it with leaves or straw. Wrap the heads in a feed bag. Cover it with more leaves or straw in the trench and cover well with soil and more mulch. Be sure to mark where you've buried them!

To keep cabbage through the winter, pull out by the roots. Turn upside down in a hole big enough so you can cover the head with dirt. Let the roots stick up into the air. This should keep until spring. Just take a hold of the roots and pull out. You can't get it when the ground is frozen, though. Be sure not to bury it when the weather is still warm. Wait until after the first frost.

STORING CARROTS

Take carrots out of the ground before the ground freezes. Put a layer of carrots in a box or bucket or some kind of container. Then cover with dirt. Alternate like that until container is full, putting dirt on top. Store in a dark cellar. Most of the carrots should stay firm until about April or May.

Cut off the top (whole end of carrots, not just the green part). Store in garbage bags. This way they keep nice and fresh and do not wrinkle. This also works nice for beets.

We like best to leave carrots in the ground for the winter. Just cover well with leaves, straw, or hay, and dig as you're ready for them. They have better flavor this way. Do not leave in the ground too long after the ground thaws out in the spring or carrots will start to rot.

WINTER TOMATOES

In the fall, when your garden still has green tomatoes that won't ripen anymore, take them inside and wrap them in newspaper and lay them on your basement floor. Do not stack them! By Christmas time you will have red tomatoes.

FOOD PRESERVATION

198

NOTES

miscellaneous

SPROUTING SEEDS▾

1 wide-mouth quart jar
piece of cheese cloth or stocking
rubber band or can ring
seeds for sprouting

Put 1 T. seeds in jar and cover with water. Soak overnight and drain. Turn upside down in a small bowl at room temperature and rinse with clean water twice a day. After a few days, set jar in the sun to increase chlorophyll and vitamin A content. It takes about a week for the can to fill, then they are ready to eat.

Note: Alfalfa sprouts are especially rich in protein and are delicious in sandwiches, salads, scrambled, eggs, hamburgers, meat loaf, sauces . . .

CREAM CHEESE

Add 1 pint buttermilk to 1 quart warm milk, and let it set 24 hours. Add 1 gallon warm milk and let it sour another 24 hours. Warm over hot water for 30 minutes, then pour into a cloth bag to drain. Let it set one hour. Salt to taste and wrap in waxed paper. It may be used immediately for sandwiches, on crackers, or in recipes calling for cream cheese. Refrigerate until used. This cream cheese can also be frozen.

KRAFT CHEESE

2 1/2 gal. skim milk

Let set until very sour and thick. Heat on burner until too hot to hold hand in (not boiling), for 20 minutes or so until curdles are very firm. Strain through cloth and squeeze very dry. Put curdles on paper towel to dry off. Mix in 1 t. baking soda. Melt in double boiler 1/2 c. butter. Mix in cheese curdles and stir until smooth and melted. Slowly add 1 c. hot sweet cream. Last of all, add 2 1/2 t. salt, or to suit taste.

The amount of cream can be altered for softer or stiffer cheese. One or two eggs may be added.

HOMEMADE CHEESE

3 gal. skim milk   1 c. plain yogurt
1 gal. whole milk   3 T. salt
1/2 t. liquid rennet in 1/2 c. cool water
blancher   cheesecloth
flat plate to fit into blancher
gal. jar that fits into blancher, full of rocks or sand

   In large pot, heat milk to 86°. Remove from heat. Mix yogurt with 1 c. heated milk and beat with wire whisk. Stir into milk. Stir rennet and water into milk. Let set 30 minutes or until well coagulated. Now set on low heat and stir frequently, until milk reaches the temperature of 100°. Remove from heat and let set another 30 minutes, stirring occasionally. Drain off whey and mix salt into curds. Put blancher on drainboard or into sink and fit with cheesecloth. Pour in curds. Draw up all corners of cheesecloth and cover top of curds, leaving as few folds as possible. On top of this, put plate and jar of rocks. Allow to press for 2 hours. Remove cheese from press, rewrap, and turn upside down. Replace plate and jar of rocks and press 22 hours more. Place finished cheese on an absorbent cloth and store in a fairly cool area (around 60°). Turn once or twice a day and grease the side you turn up with 1 t. oil for 2 weeks. Enjoy!

DRIED HERBS▼

   Ideal for basil, celery leaves, chives, parsley, and thyme, etc.
   Gather and select leaves when mature but before flowers develop. Wash thoroughly and drain; pat dry with paper towels. Chop or mince if desired.
   Note: I chop them after they've been dried. Arrange on dehydrator screens. Dry 4 - 8 hours or until brittle and easily crumbled. Store in airtight containers.

A slice of raw potato rubbed over your hands will remove vegetable stains.

A cloth dampened with vinegar and wrapped around cheese will prevent drying out.

HOMEMADE SALAMI

24 lbs. hamburger	4 t. salt
2 1/2 t. garlic powder	1 T. sage
8 T. soy sauce	1 T. thyme
3 T. dry mustard	2 T. chili powder
1 T. black pepper	

Put hamburger in large container. Add rest of ingredients and mix *thoroughly* with your hands. Cover and chill for 24 hours.

Divide into 1 - 2 lb. pieces and shape each into a firm roll. Wrap snugly in cotton cloth and tie ends securely. Put on a rack with a pan underneath, in 225° oven for 6 hours. Allow to stand a few minutes, then unwrap and blot with towel to remove any excess fat. Freeze in tin foil or bags. Thaw and refrigerate when ready to use.

Note: This is a mild recipe, as our family doesn't care for spicy things.

BEEF JERKY

Jerky is a meat that is salted, seasoned, and then dried. It is an age-old process, that is now more popular than ever.

Method:

Trim fat from 2 lbs. raw, lean beef. Slice into very thin strips, 1/8 to 1/4 inch thick. Place meat strips in a single layer in a glass or stainless steel bowl. Season to taste with salt, pepper, and liquid smoke. Repeat layers until all meat is used. Place a small saucer over meat to weight it down. Refrigerate overnight, about 10 hours. Drain. Arrange strips on dehydrator screens. Dry for 10 - 12 hours. or until leathery and no moisture is present.

Ham Jerky: Prepare thin slices of fully cooked ham as directed above.

CHOCOLATE SYRUP

To keep on hand for chocolate milk or to dribble over frozen bananas at the table.

3 c. honey
3 T. carob
1 t. vanilla

1/2 c. water
1/2 t. salt

Heat to combine, then store in refrigerator.

GARDEN TEA CONCENTRATE

Bring 4 qt. water to a boil. Remove from heat and add 4 cups fresh tea leaves. Cover and let set for 20 minutes. Remove leaves, sweetener may be added if you wish. Cool and freeze. To serve mix one part concentrate and two parts water, or to suit your taste.

A DELICIOUS DRINK▾

1 part grape juice
2 parts apple juice

APPLE YOGURT DRINK▾

1/2 c. yogurt
pinch of cinnamon

1/2 c. apple juice

Beat well with egg beater and chill. Serves 1.

MISCELLANEOUS

EGG NOG

1 egg, beaten   1/4 t. vanilla
1 glass of milk   maple syrup to taste
    This makes 1 serving. Chill and serve on a warm summer day.

SOY MILK▾

Makes 2 gal.
    Boil 15 cups of water.
    Blend till smooth:
6 cups water
1 lb. soy flour
    Stir into boiling water. Simmer 30 minutes add 15 cups sold water and chill.

QUICK PICK-ME-UP

1/4 c. honey   2 level tsp. red pepper
1/4 c. vinegar   water to make 1 qt.
    Warm it up so it mixes well. Sip on it for flues and colds or a quick energy giver.

HOMEMADE BAKING POWDER

    (When you want to avoid the aluminum contained in most commercial baking powders.)
2 c. Arrowroot powder   2 c. cream of tartar
1 c. sodium bicarbonate (baking soda)
    Sift together several times. Use as any other baking powder.

HERB CROUTONS

4 T. butter

4 slices bread, cubed

parsley

all purpose Parsley Patch seasoning

garlic salt

sesame seeds

   Melt butter in large frying pan. Toss in bread cubes. Add parsley and seasonings. Keep stirring cubes occasionally while crisping on low – about 10 min. Delicious!

PEANUT BUTTER SPREAD FOR CHURCH

4 c. whole wheat flour (add raw)

1 1/2 - 2 qts. water thickened with corn starch

10 lbs. peanut butter

8 c. hot water

6 c. sorghum

6 c. honey

salt to taste

   Mix altogether. Refrigerate leftover spread, it will not keep long at room temperature.

PLAY DOUGH

1/2 c. salt

2 t. cream of tartar

1 T. oil

1 c. wheat flour

1 c. water

grated crayons or food coloring

   In a pan mix dry ingredients then add wet ingredients. Turn on low heat. Stir constantly till until mixture gets rubbery. Add grated crayons or food coloring when it starts to get warm. When dough comes together, turn out on table and knead a little.

MISCELLANEOUS

Garlic is good in most soups, salads, sauces, meats, fish, and casseroles.

Dip fruit slices in pure lemon juice to keep them from becoming brown.

Sesame seeds can be added to pancakes, quick breads, biscuits, and salad dressings, or rice.

Don't boil herbal teas. Bring water to boiling point, then take off of fire and place leaves in it. For best flavor and light color, steep only 5 minutes.

When buying dried fruits, be sure they are unsulphured.

If you want juice for a picnic, freeze it the night before in a plastic jug. Put it in your cooler when packing and it will keep the food cold. The juice will melt enough to pour by picnic time.

If your herbs and spices are losing their flavor, try putting them in freezer bags. Place them in freezer boxes and freeze them. You can keep a small amount on your spice rack for current use, while the larger amounts stay fresh.

For an excellent mouthwash mix together 1 t. baking soda, 1 t. salt, and 1 t. vinegar.

If you feel keyed up at bedtime, 1/2 t. honey may help you relax.

Metal Band-Aid boxes or pill bottles are handy for storing small items such as pins, buttons, and rubber bands. Label them so you know at a glance what the contents are. You can stack them or store them in drawers.

Use a long-handled mop to wash the top part of walls and ceilings. You'll be able to reach up high and give it a good scrubbing and there's no danger of falling off a ladder or stool while you work.

Salt or baking soda on small fires will smother it.

To remove paint spots on clothing, use ammonia and turpentine (equal amounts) several times, then wash thoroughly.

Add some cornstarch to hot vinegar water to wash windows. It will wipe easier and sparkle more and is not as harsh as ammonia.

Use 1 t. baking soda to a pint of water to remove stains from plastic kitchenware.

To ward off tomato hornworms, sprinkle cornmeal around plant.

MISCELLANEOUS

NOTES

natural
food resources

AMERICAN ORSA INC.

P.O. Box 189, Redmond, Utah 84652 • (801) 529-7487

"Real Salt" is a natural mineral rock salt which has not been heated and has no preservatives or additives.

BARCELONA NUT COMPANY

500 S. Fulton Ave., Baltimore, MD 21223 • (410) 233-5252 • Fax (410) 233-6555

Over sixty kinds of nut snacks. Not organic.

BASS PECAN COMPANY

PO Drawer 42, Lumberton, MS 39455 • (800) PECANSI (1-800-732-2671) • Fax (601) 796-3630

Pecans.

BERMUDA KNOLL PECANS

Rt. 1 Box 59, Montezuma, GA 31063 • (912) 472-7983

Organically grown. Available October through February or March.

BLUE HERON FARMS

PO Box 68, Rumsey, CA 95679 • (916) 796-3799

Certified organic walnuts and oranges. Shipped only in season.

CHIEFTAN WILD RICE COMPANY

PO Box 290, 1210 Basswood Ave., Spooner, WI 54801 • (800) 262-6368 • Fax (715) 635-6415

Wild rice and wild rice blends.

DELF TREE FARM

234 Union Street, North Adams, MA 01247

Certified organically grown mushrooms.

DIAMOND ORGANICS

PO Box 2159, Freedom, CA 95019 • (800) 433-3998

Fresh fruits and vegetables organically grown. Expensive but top quality.

DOUBLE J FARMS

7157 State Hwy. 81, Platteville, WI 53818

Economical source of herbs for seasoning.

EAST DOVER SUGAR

5423 E. Dover Road, Clare, MI 48617 • (517) 386-3162

Maple syrup.

FIDDLER'S GREEN FARM

PO Box 254, RFD 1 Box 656, Belfast, ME 04915 • Ph/Fax (800) 729-7935

Baking mixes, whole grain cereals, flours, grains, jams, honey, syrup.

THE FOWLER'S MILLING COMPANY

12500 Fowlers Mill Road, Chardon, OH 44024

Baking mixes and scratch baking ingredients without preservatives. Honey products, fruit spreads, raspberry products, herbs, pickled vegetables.

FRANKFERD FARMS FOOD

717 Saxonburg Blvd., Saxonburg, PA 16056 • (412) 352-9500 • Fax (412) 352-9510

Soy products, yogurt, cheese, dried fruit, nuts, seeds, grains, beans, cereal, pasta, soups, juice, nut butters, oil, grain syrup, honey, dressings, organic produce – fresh and frozen.

GARDEN SPOT

438 White Oak Road, New Holland, PA 17557 • (717) 354-4936 or (800) 829-5100

Baking supplies, beverages, cereals, flours, grains, cheese, yogurt, non-dairy desserts, fruits and vegetables – dried, frozen or fresh, meat and poultry, nuts, pasta, seeds, spreads, sweeteners.

GENESEE NATURAL FOODS

R.D. #2 Box 105, Genesee, PA 16923 • (814) 228-3200

Mostly certified and organically grown. Always chemical free. Bread, cheese, juice, snacks, cereals, jams, teas, honey, pasta, soy products, beans, rice, sauces, vitamins, soups, flour, grain, herbs.

GOLD MINE NATURAL FOODS

3419 Hancock Street, San Diego, CA 92110-4307 • (800) 475-Food • Fax (619) 296-9756 • Customer Service (619) 296-8536

Beans, beverages, grain, food processors, household products.

HEARTLAND FOODS

RD 2 Box 189B, Susquehanna, PA 18847 • (717) 879-8790

Organic beans, breads, cereals, dried fruit, grains, nuts, oils, pasta, beverages, herbs, cheese.

KING ARTHUR FLOUR BAKER'S CATALOG

PO Box 876, Norwich, VT 05055 • (800) 827-6836 • Fax (800) 343-3002

Full line of organic flour, grain, baking tools, and baking equipment.

LEGUMES PLUS

PO Box 380, Fairfield, WA 99012 • (800) 845-1349 • Fax (509) 283-2314

Seventeen kinds of lentil soup. You will pay more for quality packages.

LOS CHILEROS DE NUEVO MEXICO

PO Box 6215, Santa Fe, NM 87502

Chiles, cornmeal, mexican sauces.

McFADDEN FARMS

Potter Valley, CA 95469 • (707) 743-1122 or 1-800-343-5636

Garlic and wild rice.

MORNINGLAND DAIRY

6248 CR 2980, Mountain View, MO 65548 • (417) 469-3817 • Fax (417) 469-5086

Cheese made of unpasteurized milk and vegetable rennet.

MOUNTAIN ARK TRADING COMPANY

PO Box 3170, Fayetteville, AR 72702

Nice variety of whole grains, pasta, nuts, beans, sauces, dried foods, herbs and other health aids. New age all the way through.

NATURAL WAY MILLS

Route 2 Box 37, Middle River, MN 56737 • (218) 222-3677 • (800) 372-3677 • Fax (218) 222-3408

Organically grown whole grains, flours, and cereals.

NATURE'S

4860 E. Main Street, Berlin, OH 44610 • (330) 893-2605

One hundred and fifty varieties of herbs, spices, natural baking supplies, nuts, grains, dried fruits, cereals. One of the finest sources we've used.

THE ORIENTAL PANTRY

423 Great Road, Acton, MA 01720

Oriental foods, flavorings and cookbooks with all the kitchen gadgets you need to prepare it. Featuring China, Japan, Thailand, India and Philippines.

P-R FARMS, INC.

2917 E. Shepherd Ave., Clovis, CA 93612

Almonds.

PHIPPS RANCH

PO Box 349, Pescadero, CA 94060 • (415) 879-0787 • (415) 879-16722 • (800) 279-0889

Forty kinds of beans.

RICHARD'S MAPLE PRODUCTS

545 Water Street, Chardon, OH 44024 • (330) 286-4160

Pure maple syrup.

RIVER VALLEY CHEESE

PO Box 377, Lanesboro, MN 55949 • (507) 467-7000

Cheese made with BGH free milk.

GERALD SCHMIEDICKE

5423 E. Dover Road, Clare, MI 48617

Maple syrup all year long.

SOUTH TEX ORGANICS

6 Betty Drive, Mission, TX 78572 • (210) 585-1040 • Fax (210) 581-1040

Citrus fruits.

STARR ORGANIC PRODUCE

PO Box 561502, Miami, FL 33256-1502 • (305) 262-1242 • Fax (305) 262-5317

Grapefruit, oranges, tangelos, tangerines, papayas, avocados, apple-bananas, mangos.

TROYER'S WHOLESOME FOODS

8934 CR 320, Holmesville, OH 44633 • (330) 279-9222

Certified organic Saskatchawan whole wheat grain in bulk.

VIRGINIA HONEY COMPANY INC.

PO Box 246, Berryville, VA 22611 • (703) 955-1304

Honey, molasses, preserves, jellies, apple butter.

WATKINS

150 Liberty Street, PO Box 5570, Winona, MN 55987-0570

Spices, extracts, environment friendly cleaners, lotions and soaps.

WALNUT ACRES ORGANIC FARMS

Penns Creek, PA 17862 • (800) 433-3998

Established 1946. Cereals, baking mixes, fresh fruits and vegetables, soups, poultry, beef, flour, whole grains, nuts, fruit spread, juices, dried fruit, pure oils, rice, seeds and sprouts, cheeses, dried beans 100% organic, no additives.

WOOD PRAIRIE FARM

RFD 1 Box 164, Bridgewater, ME 04735 • (207) 429-9765 • (800) 239-9765

Certified organic potatoes of all kinds.

YE OLDE GRIST MILL

129 S. Swinehart Road, Orrville, OH 44667 • (330) 683-0377

All kinds of natural stone ground flour, breading mix.

NATURAL FOOD
RESOURCES

216

NOTES

index

Bread

100% WHOLE WHEAT BREAD 4
APPLE CORN BREAD 18
APPLE RAISIN OATMEAL MUFFINS . 13
BANANA BREAD 16
BANANA MUFFINS 14
BARLEY BREAD 7
BRAN MUFFINS 11
BRAN MUFFINS▼ 10
BUTTERMILK BISCUITS 10
CAROL'S WHOLE WHEAT BREAD . . . 3
CARROT MUFFINS 14
CINNAMUFFINS 12
CORN BREAD 19, 20
CORN BREAD▼ 19
CORN PONE 20
CORNMEAL BISCUITS▼ 9
CORNMEAL MUFFINS 12
CREAM PUFFS▼ 21
CRUSTY CORNBREAD 18
DELICIOUS QUICK BREAD 17
DELICIOUS ROLLS 8
EASY NO-KNEAD WHOLE WHEAT
    BREAD 4
FAVORITE BRAN MUFFINS 11
GLUTEN-FREE BISCUITS▼ 10
GLUTEN-FREE CORNBREAD▼ 19

HEALTHY MUFFINS▼ 14
HOVIS BREAD 8
LIGHT AND CRUSTY BREAD 2
MULTI-GRAIN BREAD 5
OATMEAL BREAD 6
OATMEAL BUNS 9
ORANGE NUT BREAD 15
ORANGE OATMEAL MUFFINS 12
OUR BEST WHEAT BREAD 2
PLUCKETS 7
PUMPKIN BREAD 17
PUMPKIN BREAD▼ 16
QUICK AND LIGHT DINNER ROLLS . . 9
QUICK MUFFINS 15
RICE BREAD▼ 6
SOURDOUGH STARTER 21
SPOON BREAD▼ 20
SWEDISH RYE BREAD (2 LOAVES) . . . 5
WHOLE GRAIN PUMPKIN MUFFINS . 13
WHOLE WHEAT BREAD 3
ZUCCHINI BREAD 17

Breakfasts

3-GRAIN CEREAL 38

218

INDEX

BAKED OATMEAL 36
BEST GRANOLA 35
BRAN CAKES 27
BREAKFAST YOGURT 34
BUCKWHEAT PANCAKES▼ 28, 29
BUTTERMILK GRAPENUTS 31
BUTTERMILK PANCAKES 25
CHEESE SOUFFLE 33
CIDER SNITZ (UNSWEETENED)▼ . . . 32
CORN MUSH 25
CORN MUSH PANCAKES 29
CORNMEAL MUSH 25
CORNMEAL WAFFLES▼ 24
EGG DUTCH 33
FRIED OAT CEREAL 35
FRUIT SYRUP 32
GRANOLA 35, 36
GRANOLA▼ 36
GRANOLA BREAKFAST CEREAL 37
GRAPENUTS 31
OATMEAL BUCKWHEAT PANCAKES . .
. . . . 26
OATMEAL PANCAKES 26
OATMEAL PANCAKES▼ 26
OLD FASHIONED BUCKWHEAT
        PANCAKES 28
OMELET 34
PANCAKE MIX▼ 30
PEANUT BUTTER GRANOLA 38
QUICK FRIED MUSH▼ 24
SCRAMBLED EGGS 33
SCRAPPLE 33
SOFT BOILED EGGS▼ 34
SPICY UNBAKED GRANOLA 37
WAFFLE OR PANCAKE TOPPINGS▼ . 30
WAFFLES▼ 26
WHEAT MUSH 24
WHOLE GRAIN PANCAKE MIX 30

WHOLE GRAIN PANCAKES▼ 27
ZUCCHINI PANCAKES 32

Cakes ·

ANGEL FOOD CAKE 134
APPLE CAKE 127
APPLESAUCE CAKE 127
AUTUMN SURPRISE CAKE 124
BANANA CHIFFON CAKE 133
BANANA CREME FROSTING 136
BEST GINGERBREAD 132
BUTTER CREAM FROSTING 136
CAROB BLACK CRACK CAKE 120
CAROB FROSTING 135
CAROB FUDGE FROSTING 135
CAROB OATMEAL CAKE 119
CAROB POTATO CAKE 121
CARROT CAKE 130
COCONUT ICING 135
COFFEE CAKE 122
CREAM CHEESE FROSTING 136
DOUBLE DELIGHT 131
FATHER'S CHOICE CAKE 125
FROSTING 138
FRUIT CAKET 134
GERMAN CRUMB CAKE 120
GLORIFIED GINGERBREAD 132
HONEY APPLESAUCE CAKE 126
HONEY ICING 137
HONEY LEMON SAUCE 138
LEMON CAKE FILLING 138
LEMON PUDDING CAKE 123
MARBLE CAKE 118
MOIST BANANA FRUIT CAKE 125
MOLASSES CAKE 126

NUTRITION CAKE 128
ORANGE SYRUP 137
PEANUT BUTTER BRAN CAKE 121
PEAR SAUCE DELIGHT CAKE 128
PINEAPPLE CAKE 129
PINEAPPLE CARROT CAKE▼ 131
PINEAPPLE SHEET CAKE 126
PUMPKIN CAKE 122
ROLLED OATS CAKE 118
SPICE OATMEAL CAKE 119
SPICY GRANOLA CAKE 123
STEAMED GRAHAM CAKE 134
SUGAR FREE ICING 137
SUGAR FREE ORANGE ICING▼ . . . 137
WACKY CAKE 129
WHOLE WHEAT ANGEL FOOD CAKE . .
. . . . 133
WHOLE WHEAT CHOCOLATE CAKE . .
. . . . 128
ZUCCHINI FUDGE CAKE 124

Cookies

BANANA CUPCAKES 114
BLUEBERRY SNACKING BARS 110
CAROB BROWNIES▼ 112
CAROB SQUARES 112
CARROT OATMEAL COOKIES 96
CINNAMON ZUCCHINI BROWNIES . .
. . . . 114
DANISH APPLE BARS▼ 111
DELICIOUS HEALTH BARS 108
FIG BRAID 115
FUDGE NUT BARS 107
GINGER COOKIES 102
GINGERSNAPS 102
GRANOLA BARS (UNSWEETENED)▼ . .
. . . . 109
GRANOLA COOKIES 97
GREAT GRANOLA BARS 110
HI-PROTEIN ENERGY BARS 109
MAPLE BARS 104
MATRIMONY SQUARES 113
MINCEMEAT BARS 104
MOLASSES COOKIES 99
MOM'S DELIGHT (LIKE BROWNIES) . .
. . . . 113
NO-SUGAR COOKIES 100
NUTRITION BARS 108
OATMEAL BARS (UNSWEETENED)▼ . . .
. . . . 105
OATMEAL COCONUT BARS 105
OATMEAL FRUIT COOKIES▼ 96
PEANUT BUTTER BARS 106
PEANUT BUTTER COOKIES 97
PUMPKIN COOKIES 101
RAISIN BARS 111
RAISIN CRISP 111
SANDWICH COOKIES 102
SORGHUM COOKIES 98, 99
SOUR CREAM COOKIES 98
SUGARLESS COOKIES▼ 101
TOASTED OAT BARS 106
WHEAT AND OATMEAL COOKIES . . 97
WHOOPIE PIE COOKIES 103
WHOOPIE PIES 103

Desserts

APPLE CRISP 150
APPLE CRUMBLE 150
APPLE CRUNCH 151
APPLE GOODIE 152

BANANA PINEAPPLE CRISP 155
BROWN BETTY 153
CAROB CORNSTARCH PUDDING . 156
CHERRY PUDDING 155
COOKED APPLES 154
COTTAGE CHEESE PUDDING 156
CREAM CHEESE DESSERT 161
DANISH RASPBERRY PUDDING . . . 157
DATE PUDDING 157, 158
FLUFFY TAPIOCA CREAM 154
FRUIT GOODIE▼ 151
PEACH CRISP▼ 153
PUMPKIN CUSTARD 159
PUMPKIN PUDDING 160
RICE PUDDING 158, 159
SPICED APPLES 154
STEAMED GRAHAM PUDDING . . . 160
STRAWBERRY SHORTCAKE 161
SUMMER FRUIT COBBLER 152
TAPIOCA PUDDING 160
TEN DOLLAR FRUIT PIE 153
YOGURT RICE PUDDING 159

CHEEZ WHIZ TO CAN 188
COLE SLAW TO CAN 193
CUCUMBER CARROT RELISH 190
DRESSING MIX▼ 187
FREEZING PEAS 196
FRUIT JELLY▼ 192
GREEN TOMATO MINCEMEAT . . . 188
HOMEMADE SAUERKRAUT 194
HONEY VINEGAR 193
HOT PEPPER SAUCE▼ 189
KETCHUP 187
MINESTRONE 186
PICKLE RELISH 189
PICKLED BEETS 191
PIZZA SAUCE▼ 187
SALT AND SUGAR-FREE PICKLES . . . 190
STORING CABBAGE 196
STORING CARROTS 197
TO CAN RED BEETS 191
VEGETABLE SOUP 186
WINTER TOMATOES 197

Food Preservation

APPLE BUTTER 192
APPLE BUTTER▼ 193
APPLE JELLY 192
BEAN SOUP 186
BERRY JAM 191
CANNED HAMBURGER 195
CANNED PEARS 195
CANNING STRAWBERRIES WITH
    TAPIOCA 188

Ice Cream and Frozen Desserts

ALMOND ICE CREAM 167
APPLE DATE SMOOTHIE▼ 167
APRICOT-PEACH SMOOTHIE▼ . . . 168
BANANA ICE CREAM 165
BANANA SPLIT 170
BLUEBERRY SMOOTHIE▼ 167
DAIRY QUEEN ICE CREAM 165
DELICIOUS ICE CREAM 164
FROZEN FRUIT 168
FROZEN STRAWBERRY DESSERT . . . 168

HONEY ICE CREAM 166

HOT BLUEBERRY SAUCE 170

ICE CREAM 164

ICE CREAM SANDWICHES 170

ICE MILK 165

NUTRITIOUS ICE CREAM 165

ORANGE SHERBET 169

ORANGE SLUSH 169

PEACH ICE CREAM 166

PINEAPPLE SHAKE 169

Main Dishes

4-LAYER MEAL 40

BAKED BEANS 56

BAKED CARROTS 52

BAKED CHICKEN PIE 62

BAKED CRACKER CRUMB POTATOES▾
. . . . 64

BAKED POTATO STICKS▾ 64

BAKED RICE▾ 46

BAKED SAUERKRAUT 52

BARBECUE LENTILS 57

BARBECUE SAUCE 71

BARBECUED CHICKEN 58

BEAN SOUP 71

BOSTON BAKED BEANS 56

BREAD STUFFING 54

BREAD TOPPING 69

BROCCOLI SOUP 72

BROWN RICE AND CHICKEN▾ 48

BROWN RICE WITH ZUCCHINI SAUCE▾
. . . . 46

BURRITOS 66

BUSY MOTHER CASSEROLE▾ 40

CARROT NUT LOAF 53

CHICKEN AND RICE▾ 48

CHICKEN BREASTS 58

CHICKEN FRITTERS 53

CHICKEN TURNOVERS▾ 59

CHILI SOUP 73

CHINESE GLOB 63

CHOP SUEY 49

CORN FRITTERS▾ 67

CREAM OF CELERY SOUP 73

CREAM OF CHICKEN SOUP 75

CREAMY POTATO SOUP 74

CRUNCHY CHICKEN 60

DANDELION GRAVY 69

DELICIOUS BROWN GRAVY 69

DELICIOUS CABBAGE STEW▾ 43

DELICIOUS FRIED BROWN RICE . . . 47

DELICIOUS TOFU SOUP 76

DINNER IN A DISH▾ 42

DRESSED-UP STEAK 54

EASIEST SPLIT PEA SOUP 71

EASY BEAN AND LENTIL CASSEROLE . .
. . . . 40

EGGPLANT PATTIES 55

EL RANCHO CASSEROLE 41

FAMILY FAVORITE ZUCCHINI 50

FARMER'S DELIGHT CASSEROLE . . . 41

FRIED RICE▾ 47

GRATED POTATO CASSEROLE 44

HAMBURGER CUPCAKES 58

HAY STACKS 45

HOMEMADE MUSHROOM SOUP . . 72

HOMEMADE TACOS▾ 67

HOT CHICKEN SANDWICHES 65

ITALIAN MEATBALLS (NO MEAT) . . 65

KALE - LENTIL SOUP▾ 72

LENTIL RICE SOUP▾ 74

LENTILBURGERS 53

MEATBALL PIZZA 65

222

INDEX

MEATLESS POTATO SOUP 76
MILLET SOUP 74
MOCK COUNTRY SAUSAGE 59
MOM'S MEAT LOAF 55
MUSHROOM SOUP 73
NO NAME CASSEROLE 44
OATMEAL DRESSING▼ 68
OKRA AND TOMATOES▼ 52
ONE DISH MEAL 42
OVEN-FRIED MUSTARD CHICKEN . 59
POTATO KUGEL 62
PERFECT BROWN RICE▼ 48
PIZZA CRUST▼ 61
PIZZA DOUGH 61
RICE CASSEROLE 49
RICE MEATBALL STEW 63
RICE PIZZA 61
RICE-VEGETABLE CASSEROLE▼ 64
RICE/LEGUME CASSEROLET 47
SAVORY EGG PUFF 68
SESAME RICE▼ 49
SKILLET MEAL▼ 42
SOUR CREAM FOR BAKED POTATOES .
. . . . 71
SPRING PEAS AND POTATOES 44
TACOS OR TORTILLAS 67
TACOS▼ 66
THREE SISTERS CASSEROLE 45
TIME SAVER SUNDAY DINNER 63
TOMATO GRAVY 70
TOMATO SOUP 75
TOMATO SOUP▼ 75
TURKEY POT PIE 43
TVP BURGERS 57
VEGETABLE PIZZA 60
WHITE SAUCE 70
YUMMY HAMBURGERS 60

ZUCCHINI CASSEROLE 51
ZUCCHINI FRITTERS▼ 51
ZUCCHINI HAMBURGER BAKE 51
ZUCCHINI STICKS 50
ZUCCHINI VEGETABLE DISH 50

Miscellaneous

A DELICIOUS DRINK▼ 203
APPLE YOGURT DRINK▼ 203
BEEF JERKY 202
CHOCOLATE SYRUP 203
CREAM CHEESE 200
DRIED HERBS▼ 201
EGG NOG 204
GARDEN TEA CONCENTRATE . . . 203
HERB CROUTONS 205
HOMEMADE BAKING POWDER . . . 204
HOMEMADE CHEESE 201
HOMEMADE SALAMI 202
KRAFT CHEESE 200
PEANUT BUTTER SPREAD FOR
        CHURCH 205
PLAY DOUGH 205
QUICK PICK-ME-UP 204
SOY MILK▼ 204
SPROUTING SEEDS▼ 200

Pies

ALL-BRAN PIE CRUST▼ 146
APPLE PIE▼ 141
BARLEY PIE CRUST▼ 147
BLACKBERRY CUSTARD PIE 141

CAROB PIE 142
COCONUT CREAM PIE 140
COCONUT PIE SHELL▼ 147
CREAM CHEESE PIE 140
CRUST FOR DESSERTS▼ 146
DELICIOUS WHOLE WHEAT PASTRY
    CRUST 146
GRANOLA PIE CRUST 147
HONEY PIE 143
IMPOSSIBLE PUMPKIN PIE 144
NUT PIE SHELL 148
OATMEAL PIE 143
OATMEAL PIE CRUST 147
PEACH AND PRALINE PIE 142
PIE CRUST 148
PIE DOUGH 148
PUMPKIN PIE 144
RICE PIE CRUST 148
SPICY PUMPKIN PIE 145
STRAWBERRY CREAM PIE 141
WHOLE WHEAT PASTRY 145

Salads and Dressings

APPLE PEAR SALAD 84
APPLE SALAD 85
APPLE-CABBAGE SLAW 79
BLENDER MAYONNAISE▼ 87
CARROT SALAD 83
COLESLAW DRESSING▼ 92
COOKED DRESSING 88
COTTAGE CHEESE DRESSING▼ . . . 88
COTTAGE CHEESE SALAD 94
CUCUMBER DRESSING▼ 88

EASY CABBAGE SLAW 78
FRENCH DRESSING 89
FRUIT DIP▼ 92
FRUIT SALAD GELATIN 84
HEALTH SALAD 84
HEALTHY HAYSTACK▼ 79
HEALTHY POTATO SALAD 82
HEALTHY VEGETABLE DIP▼ 92
HOMEMADE MIRACLE WHIP 86
LETTUCE DRESSING 89
MAKE-AHEAD SALAD 81
MAYONNAISE 87
MEXICAN SALAD DRESSING 89
MIXED BEAN SALAD 78
OIL DRESSING (FOR LETTUCE SALAD)
    90
ORANGE SALAD 83
PAPRIKA DIP 92
PINEAPPLE DIP 93
POTATO SALAD▼ 82
POTATO SUPPER SALAD 82
QUICK ORANGE JELLO 83
RAINBOW FRUIT SALAD 85
RICE SALAD 80
SALAD DRESSING 91
SALAD EGGS 81
SANDWICH SPREAD▼ 86
SOYBEAN - CHEESE SALAD 80
SPECIAL SALAD 86
STUFFED EGGS▼ 81
STUFFED PEPPERS▼ 79
STUFFED TOMATOES 78
SWEET AND SOUR DRESSING 90
THOUSAND ISLAND DRESSING . . . 91
TOMATO DIP 93
TOMATO DRESSING 90
VEGETABLE DIP 93

VINEGAR ONIONS 80

Wholesome Snacks

ALMOND OR PEANUT BUTTER BALLS .
. . . . 173
BREADSTICKS FOR TODDLERS . . . 177
CAROB OATMEAL CANDY 174
CHEESE BALL 172
CHEESE STICKS 176
CHEWY CHARLIES 175
CHILDREN'S GARDEN MIX 176
CREAM CHEESE BALLS 172
DANDY CANDY▼ 174
DATE BALLS 175
FRUIT LEATHER▼ 180
GRAHAM CRACKERS 178
OATMEAL CANDY COOKIES 174
PEANUT BUTTER BALLS▼ 172
PEANUT BUTTER FUDGE 173
PEANUT BUTTER POPCORN 175
PLAYGROUND SNACK MIX 176
POPCORN CRUNCH 173
SOFT WHOLE WHEAT PRETZELS . . . 179
TEETHING BISCUITS, CRACKERS,
        OR BREADSTICKS 177
"WHITE" CRACKERS 178

Yogurt

CARAMEL YOGURT 184
CAROL'S YOGURT▼ 182
FROZEN YOGURT 183
HOMEMADE YOGURT▼ 183
YOGURT CREAM CHEESE▼ 184
YOGURT WITH FROZEN FRUIT . . . 183
YOGURT WITH FRUIT▼ 182
YOGURT▼ 182

AUTHENTIC AMISH COOKING

The Wooden Spoon Cookbook

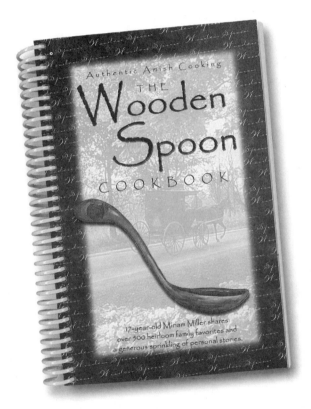

Meet 17-year-old Miriam Miller in the Wooden Spoon Cookbook. In addition to sharing her own, her mother's, and her grand-mother's favorite recipes, Miriam shares childhood memories, stories, and personal details of her life as a young Amish girl.

$10.95

· 5¹/₂" x 8¹/₂" · 194 pp · Spiral bound · Laminated cover · Double indexed
· ISBN 1-890050-41-5

Mary Yoder's Candy & Confections Cookbook

VOLUME I

Mary Yoder

Ready for a really special treat . . . one that will satisfy your sweet tooth? Dripping chocolates, dreamy fudges, reach-for-more mints, and over 100 other sweet secrets—the homemade way. Mary has over 30 years' experience in making candy and confections—for her family as well as commercially. In this book she shares her own secret recipes, never before published.

Mary Yoder's Candy and Confections Cookbook is even more! Take a good look, for example, at the 24 color photos of the author's childhood memories and unique hobbies. You'll enjoy a walk down memory lane with her through the photos of her home, gardens, and hobbies. 70 illustrations in her own original pencil art are scattered throughout the book.

The next time you need a treat so special, so unique, so mouthwatering that it can't be bought, reach for Mary Yoder's Candy and Confections Cookbook. You'll add that personal touch that's just right.

You'll make that special moment even sweeter!

$9.95

· 5^1/$_2$" x 8^1/$_2$" · 126 pp · Spiral Bound · 24 Color Photographs
· 70 Original Pencil Illustrations by Mary Yoder · ISBN 1-890050-36-9

Cooking with the
Horse & Buggy People

A Collection of Over 600 Favorite Recipes from the Heart of Holmes County

OUR MOST POPULAR COOKBOOK

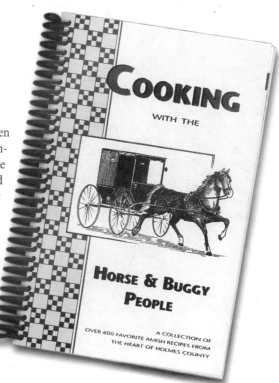

From mouth watering Amish style main dishes to kitchen dream desserts, this one has it all. Over 600 made-from-scratch recipes that please the appetite and are easy on the food budget. You'll get a whole section on canning and food preparation. The Amish, long known for their originality in the kitchen, share their favorites with you. If you desire originality, if you respect authenticity, if the Amish style cooking satisfies your taste palate—**Cooking With The Horse & Buggy People** is for you.

Contains 14 Complete Sections:
Breads, Cakes, Cookies, Desserts, Pies, Salads, Main Dishes, Soups, Cereal, Candy, Miscellaneous, Drinks, Canning, Home Remedies & Preparing Wild Game, Index.

$10.95

· 5^1/$_2$" x 8^1/$_2$" · 275 pp · Spiral Bound · Laminated Cover
· Convenient Thumb Index · ISBN 1-890050-16-4

Cooking with the Horse & Buggy People

Sample Page

H enry and Amanda Mast, authors and compilers of Cooking with the Horse and Buggy People Volume II (as well as Volume I), live close to Charm, Ohio. Their home place is in the heart of the world's largest Amish community. The Masts and their friends worked countless hours in the kitchen to perfect the 600 recipes they chose to share with the rest of the world. And it's not just the hours … think of the thousands of pots and pans that have been washed, the tables that were cleared, and the kitchen floors swept over the last ten, twenty, thirty, and even forty years to "test" and perfect these recipes. And not only that … imagine the young girl's source of delight because "Mom has made my favorite pie." Think of all the growing farm boys who have devoured mashed potatoes and dressing (an Amish staple) and licked their chops as the homemade ice cream was passed. Imagine all the grubby little fingers that have reached cautiously into the cookie jar, all the while having an ear and eye over their shoulder.

Good food. Laughter. Compliments. Memories. That's what this new volume of *Cooking with the Horse and Buggy People* is about.

$10.95

· 5¹/₂" x 8¹/₂" · 320 pp · Spiral bound
· Extra-heavy laminated cover · ISBN 1-890050-62-8

TO ORDER COOKBOOKS

Check your local bookstore or call **1-800-852-4482.**

2673 TR 421
Sugarcreek, OH 44681

Carlisle Press
WALNUT CREEK